Table of Contents

2

Main Idea: Iguanodon

Millions of years ago, many kinds of dinosaurs roamed Earth. The name of one kind of dinosaur was Iguanodon (ee-gwan-eh-don). The Iguanodon looked like a giant lizard. It had tough skin. The Iguanodon's skin must have felt like leather! Iguanodons ate plants.

Directions: Answer these questions about Iguanodons.

1. Circle the main idea:

   The Iguanodon's skin was like leather.

   The Iguanodon was a plant-eating dinosaur with tough skin.

2. What kind of food did Iguanodons eat?

   _____

3. What animal living today did the Iguanodon look like?

   _____

Making Inferences: Dining Dinosaurs

Brontosaurus dinosaurs lived in the swamps. Swamps are water areas where many plants grow. Here are the names of the other kinds of dinosaurs that lived in the swamps: Diplodocus (dip-low-dock-us), Brachiosaurus (bracky-o-saur-us), and Cetiosaurus (set-e-o-saur-us). These dinosaurs had small heads and small brains. They weighed 20 tons or more. They grew to be 60 feet long! These animals did not need to have sharp teeth.

Directions: Answer these questions about Brontosaurus and other big dinosaurs.

1. These big dinosaurs did not have sharp teeth. What did they eat?

   _____

2. Why were swamps a good place for these big dinosaurs to live?

   _____

   _____

3. These big dinosaurs had small brains. Do you think they were smart? Why?

   _____

   _____

4. Name the three kinds of dinosaurs that lived in swamps.

   _____

   _____

One of the biggest dinosaurs was Tyrannosaurus rex (ty-ran-oh-saur-us recks). This dinosaur walked on its two big back legs. It had two small, short front legs. From the top of its head to the tip of its tail, Tyrannosaurus rex measured 50 feet long. Its head was four feet long! Are you taller than this dinosaur's head? Tyrannosaurus was a meat eater. It had many small, sharp teeth. Its favorite meal was a smaller dinosaur that had a bill like a duck. This smaller dinosaur lived near water.

Directions: Answer these questions about Tyrannosaurus rex.

1. What is the story about?

   _____

2. What size was this dinosaur?

   _____

   _____

3. When this dinosaur was hungry, what did it eat?

   _____

   _____

4. Where did this dinosaur find its favorite meal?

   _____

   _____

Comprehension: Triceratops

Triceratops was one of the last dinosaurs to develop. It lived in the Cretaceous (kre-tay-shus) period of history. It was in this time that the dinosaurs became extinct. **Triceratops** means *three-horned lizard*. It was a strong dinosaur and able to defend itself well since it lived during the same time period as Tyrannosaurus rex.

Triceratops was a plant-eating dinosaur. Its body was 20 feet long, and its head, including the three horns and bony frill, was another $6\frac{1}{2}$ feet.

Directions: Answer these questions about Triceratops.

1. Dinosaurs became extinct during the _____ period of history.

2. What does **Triceratops** mean?

   _____

3. What information above tells you that Triceratops was able to defend itself?

   _____

   _____

Stegosaurus was a well-equipped fighter. It was covered with large, bony plates and had a spiked tail. As you can probably imagine, this spiked tail was a very important part of its defense. This was another large dinosaur, the same size as Triceratops. It had four legs, but the two front legs were smaller than the two hind legs, and it had a very small head compared to its body. Have you ever seen a walnut? The brain of Stegosaurus was about the same size.

Stegosaurus was one of the many plant-eating dinosaurs. You could call it a *vegetarian* (veg-e-tair-ee-un). Vegetarians only eat plants like vegetables, leaves, and grass! Stegosaurus lived in the Jurassic period, the middle era of dinosaur history.

Directions: Answer these questions about Stegosaurus.

1. Write three things that are the same size as Stegosaurus' brain.

    1)_____   2)_____   3)_____

2. The _spiked tail_ of this dinosaur was a very important part of its defense.

3. Which set of legs, the front legs or the hind ones, do you think the Stegosaurus used more? _____

    Why do you think so? _____

    _____

Recalling Details: Dinosaur Chart

Directions: Use the pages about Tyrannosaurus rex, Triceratops, and Stegosaurus to help you fill in the chart below.

	Period of History	What It Ate	Size
T. rex			
Triceratops			
Stegosaurus			

Directions: Use the chart to answer these questions.

1. Did Triceratops and Stegosaurus live on Earth at the same time?

    Yes   No

2. Which dinosaur was the largest of the three?

    _____

3. Which two of these dinosaurs were plant eaters?

    1) _____   2) _____

Like snakes, dinosaurs were cold-blooded. Cold-blooded animals cannot keep themselves warm. Because of this, dinosaurs were not very active when it was cold. In the early morning, they did not move much. When the sun grew warm, the dinosaurs became active. When the sun went down in the evening, they slowed down again for the night. The sun warmed the dinosaurs and gave them the energy they needed to move about.

Directions: Answer these questions about dinosaurs.

1. Why were dinosaurs inactive when it was cold?

_____

_____

2. What time of day were the dinosaurs active?

_____

_____

3. What times of day were the dinosaurs not active?

_____

_____

4. Why did dinosaurs need the sun?

_____

_____

Comprehension: Sizes of Dinosaurs

There were many sizes of dinosaurs. Some were as small as dogs. Others were huge! The huge dinosaurs weighed 100,000 pounds. Some dinosaurs ate meat, including other dinosaurs. Some dinosaurs, like the Iguanodon, ate only plants. Meat-eating dinosaurs had sharp teeth. Plant-eating dinosaurs had flat teeth. If you had lived long ago, would you have gotten close enough to look at their teeth?

Directions: Answer these questions about dinosaurs.

1. What size were the small dinosaurs?

   _____

2. How much did the big dinosaurs weigh?

   _____

3. Name two things the different kinds of dinosaurs ate.

   1) _____ 2) _____

4. What kind of teeth did meat-eating dinosaurs have?

   _____

5. What kind of teeth did plant-eating dinosaurs have?

   _____

Comprehension: Dinosaur Fossils

Dinosaurs roamed Earth for 125 million years. Can you imagine that much time? About 40 years ago, people found fossils of dinosaur tracks in Connecticut. Fossils are rocks that hold the hardened bones, eggs, and footprints of animals that lived long ago. The fossil tracks showed that many dinosaurs walked together in herds. The fossils showed more than 2,000 dinosaur tracks!

Directions: Answer these questions about fossils.

1. What did the people find in the fossils?

   bones eggs and footprints of animal

2. In what state were the fossils found?

   , in connecticut

3. How many tracks were in the fossils?

   2,000 dinosaur tracks!

4. What did the tracks show?

   it showed that many dinosaurs walked in herds

Main Idea: Dinosaur Models

Some people can build models of dinosaurs. The models are fakes, of course. But they are life-size and they look real! The people who build them must know the dinosaur inside and out. First, they build a skeleton. Then, they cover it with fake skin. Next, they paint it. Some models have motors in them. The motors can make the dinosaur's head or tail move. Have you ever seen a life-size model of a dinosaur?

Directions: Answer these questions about dinosaur models.

1. Circle the main idea:

   Some models of dinosaurs have motors in them.

   Some people can build life-size models of dinosaurs that look real.

2. What do the motors in model dinosaurs do?

   _____

   _____

3. What is the first step in making a model dinosaur?

   _____

   _____

4. Why do dinosaur models look real?

   _____

   _____

There are no dinosaurs alive today. They became **extinct** (ex-tinkt) millions of years ago. This was before people lived on Earth. When animals are extinct, they are gone forever. No one knows exactly why dinosaurs became extinct. Some scientists say that a disease may have killed them. Other scientists say a huge hot rock called a *comet* hit Earth. The comet caused a big fire. The fire killed the dinosaurs' food. Still, other scientists believe that Earth grew very cold. The dinosaurs died because they could not keep warm. Many scientists have ideas, but no one can know for sure exactly what happened.

Directions: Answer these questions about dinosaurs becoming extinct.

1. Why is it not possible to know what caused all the dinosaurs to die?

   _____

   _____

2. Circle the main idea:

   The dinosaurs died when a comet hit Earth and caused a big fire.

   There are many ideas about what killed the dinosaurs, but no one knows for sure.

3. What does **extinct** mean?

   _____

Recalling Details: Athletes' Nicknames

Directions: Read about nicknames. Then, solve the puzzle.

Do you have a nickname? Nicknames are the silly names people call each other. Sometimes, nicknames are mean. Usually, nicknames are nice. Most people do not mind if their friends make up a nice nickname for them. Many athletes have nicknames. Have you heard of a golfer named Tiger Woods? His real name is Eldrick. How about Babe Ruth? He was a famous baseball player for the New York Yankees in the 1920s. His real name was George.

Across:

3. Ruth's nickname

5. The silly names that people call each other

Down:

1. Tiger Woods is a _____.

2. The New York baseball team Babe Ruth played for

4. What is the nickname of Eldrick Woods?

Comprehension: Michael Phelps

Michael Phelps, a swimmer, holds the record for the most gold medals won at a single Olympic games. He competed in the Olympics in 2000, 2004, and 2008.

Michael won eight gold medals at the 2008 Olympics in Beijing, China. He has 16 medals overall, including 14 gold medals and two bronze medals. He also has an Olympic record for the most gold medals. Michael also became the youngest American male swimmer at the Olympics in 68 years when he competed at the age of 15 in 2000.

Michael trains for several hours almost every day. In order to have enough energy, Michael says he eats between 10,000 and 12,000 calories a day!

Directions: Answer these questions about Michael Phelps.

1. Circle the main idea:

   Michael trains for several hours a day.

   Michael is a record-setting Olympic athlete.

2. How many gold medals does Michael have?

   _____

3. Where did Michael win eight gold medals?

   _____

4. How many calories does Michael eat each day?

   _____

Comprehension: LeBron James

LeBron James is a professional basketball player from Ohio. His nickname is "King James," and he is 6 feet, 8 inches tall. LeBron gained attention on the basketball court as a sophomore in high school when he was named "Mr. Basketball" of Ohio.

At age 18, LeBron was selected to play for the Cleveland Cavaliers. He won the Rookie of the Year award in 2003, his first year playing basketball in the NBA. LeBron owns several records for being the youngest player to earn an achievement, including being named Rookie of the Year at age 18 and an All-Star game Most Valuable Player at age 21.

In 2007, LeBron helped the Cleveland Cavaliers advance to the NBA Finals for the first time in history. However, his team lost to the San Antonio Spurs. In 2010, LeBron left Cleveland to play for the Miami Heat.

Directions: Answer these questions about LeBron James.

1. Who is this story about?

   _____

2. For what is this athlete famous?

   _____

3. How old was LeBron when he began playing professional basketball? _____

4. What was the first NBA team that LeBron played for?

   _____

5. What achievements has LeBron earned?

   _____

Serena Williams was born September 26, 1981, in Saginaw, Michigan. When Serena was a baby, her family moved to California where she began playing tennis at age four. She began playing professionally in 1995.

Since then, Serena has won a total of 23 career Grand Slams, which include 11 singles titles, two mixed doubles, and 10 in women's doubles. The Women's Tennis Association has ranked Serena as number one in the world. She has won more career prize money than any other female athlete in history.

Serena's older sister, Venus, is also a professional tennis player. The two sisters have played against each other in 23 professional matches. Serena has won 13 of these matches. Serena and Venus also play tennis together. The pair has won 12 Grand Slam doubles titles together.

Directions: Answer these questions about Serena Williams.

1. Where was Serena born?

   _____

2. When did Serena begin playing professional tennis?

   _____

3. Who is Serena's sister?

   _____

4. When the sisters play against each other, who wins more often?

   _____

Comprehension: Lance Armstrong

You may know of Lance Armstrong. He is a famous cyclist who won the Tour de France seven times in a row. Lance set a record for the most Tour de France wins, and he earned these wins after surviving cancer!

The Tour de France is a bicycle race held every year and is said to be the most important cycling event. Riders from all over the world participate in the Tour de France. The race lasts for three weeks and covers a distance of 2,200 miles!

At age 12, Lance began his athletic career as a swimmer. He later gave up swimming to compete in a junior triathlon, which he won. At age 16, Lance became a professional triathlete. He won his first Tour de France in 1999 at age 27.

Directions: Answer these questions about Lance Armstrong.

1. Who is Lance Armstrong?

   He is a famous cyclist

2. What is the Tour de France?

   It is a bicycle race held every year

3. What other sports did Lance participate in?

   He became a swimmer Then

4. How old was Lance the first time he won the Tour de France?

   At age 27

5. How many Tour de France wins does Lance have?

   seven times in a row

Tom Brady is a football player in the NFL. He was born in 1977 in San Mateo, California. Both of his parents were sports fans and raised Tom and his three sisters to love sports, as well. As a child, Tom was a fan of the San Francisco 49ers, and his parents took him to see several football games. His favorite player was Joe Montana, a quarterback for the 49ers from 1979 to 1992.

Tom played football in college at the University of Michigan and was drafted in 2000 to play for the New England Patriots. In 1995, Tom was drafted to play baseball for the Montreal Expos, but chose football for his career path instead. So far in his football career, Tom has played in four Super Bowls. His team won three of those four Super Bowls.

Directions: Answer these questions about Tom Brady.

1. Who was Tom's favorite football player when he was a child? What was Tom's favorite team?

   _____

2. Where did Tom go to college?

   _____

3. What sport besides football was Tom good at?

   _____

4. How many Super Bowls has Tom helped win?

   _____

A great baseball champion, Babe Ruth, was born in Baltimore, Maryland, on February 6, 1895. He could hit a ball farther than most major-league players when he was only 13 years old. He did not have a very good home life, so he spent most of his early years living in a school for boys. He played baseball whenever he could, so he became very good at it.

George Ruth (his real name) was given the nickname, Babe, when he was 19 years old. A minor-league team manager, Jack Dunn, became his legal guardian. The other players on the team called him "Jack's Babe." Later, it was shortened to "Babe."

Directions: Answer these questions about Babe Ruth.

1. When was Babe Ruth born?

   _____

2. Where was he born?

   _____

3. What was Babe's original nickname?

   _____

4. How old was Babe when he got his nickname?

   _____

Babe Ruth began playing as a pitcher for the Boston Red Sox in 1915. He switched to the outfield in 1918 because his manager wanted him to bat more often. Everyone soon found out what a good hitter he was!

Yankee Stadium became known as "The House That Ruth Built," because he was such a popular player and so many people came to the baseball games. New York City was able to have a new baseball stadium because he was so popular. This left-handed baseball superstar drew large crowds to ballparks wherever his team played. Even if he didn't hit a home run, the fans were just excited to have the chance to see him.

Directions: Answer these questions about Babe Ruth.

1. Does the story let you know whether Babe is still living?

   _____ How old would he be if he were still alive?

   _____

2. What is another name for Yankee Stadium?

   _____

3. In 1915, he began playing for the _____ as a pitcher.

4. Why did his manager switch him to the outfield?

   _____

   _____

Recalling Details: The Home Run Race

The summer of 1998 was exciting for the sport of baseball. Even if you were not a big fan of this sport, you couldn't help but hear about two great sluggers—Mark McGwire and Sammy Sosa. By mid-summer, many baseball fans realized that several men were getting close to the home run record. The record of 61 home runs in a single season had been set by Roger Maris 37 years before!

On Tuesday, September 8, 1998, that record was broken. Mark McGwire, who played for the St. Louis Cardinals, hit his 62nd home run in a game with the Chicago Cubs.

To make the home run race more interesting, a player for the Chicago Cubs, Sammy Sosa, was also close to breaking the 61 home run record. On Sunday, September 13, 1998, Sammy Sosa also hit his 62nd home run.

Directions: Write the letter of the correct answer in the blanks.

A. Sept. 13   B. McGwire   C. 37

          D. Maris   E. Chicago Cubs

1. Had the home run record _____

2. First to hit 62 home runs _____

3. Sosa broke the home run record _____

4. Years record had stood _____

5. Sosa's team _____

Recalling Details: Venn Diagram

A **Venn diagram** is a diagram used to compare two things. The Venn diagram below is comparing a cat and a dog.

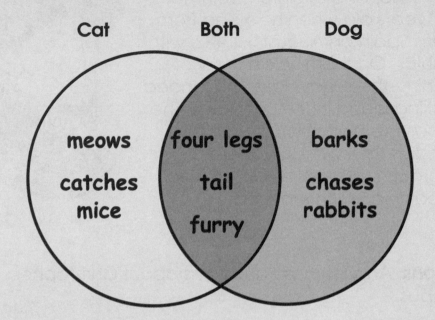

Cat	Both	Dog
meows catches mice	four legs tail furry	barks chases rabbits

Directions: Use "The Home Run Race" (page 22) to complete the Venn diagram comparing Mark McGwire and Sammy Sosa.

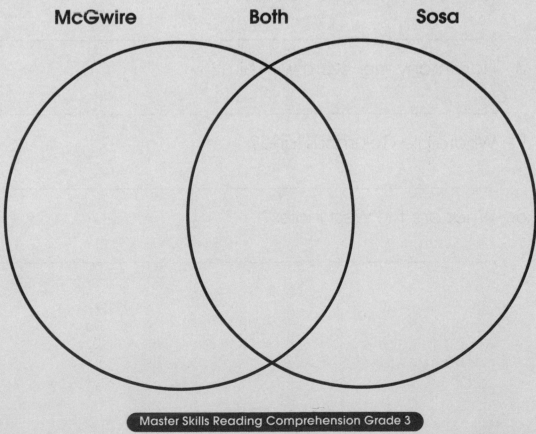

McGwire　　　　Both　　　　Sosa

What do you know about Christopher Columbus? He was a famous sailor and explorer. Columbus was 41 years old when he sailed from southern Spain on August 3, 1492, with three ships. On them was a crew of 90 men. Thirty-three days later, he landed on Watling Island in the Bahamas. The Bahamas are islands located in the West Indies. The West Indies are a large group of islands between North America and South America.

Directions: Answer these questions about Christopher Columbus.

1. How old was Columbus when he set sail from southern Spain?

   _____

2. How many ships did he take?

   _____

3. How many men were with him?

   _____

4. Where did Columbus land?

   _____

5. What are the West Indies?

   _____

Columbus was an explorer. He wanted to find out what the rest of the world looked like. He also wanted to make money! He would sail to distant islands and trade with the people there. He would buy their silks, spices, and gold. Then, he would sell these things in Spain. In Spain, people would pay high prices for them. Columbus got the queen of Spain to approve his plan. She would pay for his ships and his crew. He would keep 10 percent of the value of the goods he brought back. She would take the rest. Columbus and the queen had a business deal.

Directions: Answer these questions about Christopher Columbus.

1. Which statement is correct?

    Columbus and the queen of Spain were friends.

    Columbus and the queen of Spain were business partners.

2. Write two reasons why Columbus was an explorer.

    1) _____

    2) _____

3. What was Columbus' business deal with the queen of Spain?

    1) Columbus would get _____

    _____

    2) In return for paying his expenses, the queen would get

    _____

    _____

In 1801, President Thomas Jefferson chose an army officer named Meriwether Lewis to lead an expedition through our country's new frontier. He knew Lewis would not be able to make the journey by himself, so he chose William Clark to travel with him. The two men had known each other in the army. They decided to be co-leaders of the expedition.

The two men and a group of about 45 others made the trip from the state of Missouri, across the Rocky Mountains, all the way to the Pacific Coast. They were careful in choosing the men who would travel with them. They wanted men who were strong and knew a lot about the wilderness. It was also important that they knew some of the Native American languages.

Directions: Answer these questions about Lewis and Clark.

1. Which president wanted an expedition through the new frontier?

   _____

2. About how many people made up the entire expedition, including Lewis and Clark?

   _____

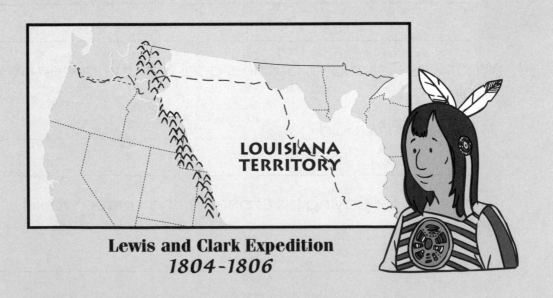

Lewis and Clark Expedition
1804-1806

LOUISIANA TERRITORY

Comprehension: Lewis and Clark

The two explorers and their men began their trip in 1804. They had camped all winter across the river from St. Louis, Missouri. While camping, they built a special boat they would need for the first part of their trip. This boat, called a *keelboat*, was 55 feet long. It could be rowed or sailed. If the men needed to use it like a raft, they could do that, too.

Besides flour, salt, and cornmeal, they took along medicines and weapons. They knew they would meet Native Americans as they traveled to the new frontier, so they also brought colored beads and other small gifts to give to them.

Directions: Answer these questions about Lewis and Clark.

1. Lewis, Clark, and the others began their trip in _____.

2. What is the name of the special boat that they built for their trip?

   _____

3. Why did they take along small gifts and colored beads?

   _____

   _____

Comprehension: Boats for the Expedition

The men were not able to take the keelboat the whole way on their trip. The Missouri River became too narrow for this boat, so Lewis and Clark had to send some of the men back to St. Louis with it. More canoes were built with the help of some friendly Native Americans. These were used for travel since they no longer had the keelboat.

Directions: Answer these questions about Lewis and Clark's boats.

1. Why couldn't Lewis and Clark use the keelboat for the entire trip?

   _____

   _____

2. What did they do with it?

   _____

3. Why did they need to build more canoes?

   _____

   _____

Find a picture of a keelboat or canoe. Draw a picture of it below.

Lewis and Clark and their men had seen large grizzly bears as they traveled through the West. They were thankful they had their weapons with them. But meeting the grizzlies was not the hardest part of the journey. It was also hard to cross the Rocky Mountains. It took the explorers and their party a month to make this part of their trip. The friendly

Shoshone tribe was very helpful in telling them how they could cross the mountains.

There were many reasons why this part of the trip was difficult. The steep, narrow pathways sometimes caused the horses to fall over the cliffs to their deaths. Many times, the men had to lead the horses. There were also fewer wild animals for the men to hunt for food.

Directions: Answer these questions about the hardships of the expedition.

1. What was the hardest part of the trip?

    _____

2. Lewis and Clark got help from which friendly Native American tribe?

    _____

3. What word in the story means *a group of people traveling together*?

    _____

New canoes had to be built for the last part of the trip. The men traveled along the Clearwater River to get to the Columbia River, and finally the Pacific Coast. They reached the Northwest Coast in November 1805.

President Jefferson was glad he had chosen Lewis and Clark to lead the expedition. They were able to make the trip successfully and could now claim the Oregon region for the United States.

Directions: Answer these questions about Lewis and Clark's expedition.

1. What two rivers did Lewis and Clark travel on the last part of their journey?

    1) _____

    2) _____

2. When did they reach the Pacific Coast? _____

3. What season of the year is that? _____

4. Circle the words below that would describe the journey:

    dangerous   quick   not planned   successful

5. This expedition allowed the United States to claim _____

    _____.

George Washington was the first president of the United States. He was born in Wakefield, Virginia, on February 22, 1732. His father was a wealthy Virginia planter. As he grew up, George Washington became interested in surveying and farming. When George was only 11 years old, his father died. George moved in with his older brother, Lawrence.

Even if he had not become the country's first president, he would have been well known because of his strong military leadership. Washington was a good leader because of his patience and his ability to survive hardships.

George Washington became president in 1789. At that time, there were only 11 states in the United States. He served two terms (four years each) as our first president. After his second term, he returned to his former home in Mt. Vernon. He died there in 1799 after catching a cold while riding around his farm in the wind and snow.

Directions: Answer these questions about George Washington.

1. In what year did George Washington become president? _____

2. Besides being our country's first president, how else did he serve our country?

_____

_____

Long ago in England, there lived a man named Robin Hood. Robin lived with a group of other men in the woods. These woods were called *Sherwood Forest*.

Robin Hood was a thief—a different kind of thief. He stole from the rich and gave what he stole to the poor. Poor people did not need to worry about going into Sherwood Forest. In fact, Robin Hood often gave them money. Rich people were told to beware. If you were rich, would you stay out of Sherwood Forest?

Directions: Answer these questions about Robin Hood.

1. What was the name of the woods where Robin Hood lived?

   _____

2. What did Robin Hood do for a living?

   _____

3. What was different about Robin Hood?

   _____

4. Did poor people worry about going into Sherwood Forest? Why or why not?

   _____

Everyone in England knew about Robin Hood. The king was mad! He did not want a thief to be a hero. He sent his men to Sherwood Forest to catch Robin Hood. But they could not catch him. Robin Hood outsmarted the king's men every time!

One day, Robin Hood sent a message to the king. The message said, "Come with five brave men. We will see who is stronger." The king decided to fool Robin Hood. He wanted to see if what people said about Robin Hood was true. The king dressed as a monk. A monk is a poor man who serves God. Then, he went to Sherwood Forest to see Robin Hood.

Directions: Circle the correct answer to these questions about the king's meeting with Robin Hood.

1. If the stories about Robin Hood were true, what happened when the king met Robin Hood?

   Robin Hood robbed the king and took all his money.

   Robin Hood helped the king because he thought he was a poor man.

2. Why didn't the king want Robin Hood to know who he was?

   He was afraid of Robin Hood.

   He wanted to find out what Robin Hood was really like.

3. Why couldn't the king's men find Robin Hood?

   Robin Hood outsmarted them.

   They didn't look in Sherwood Forest.

The king liked Robin Hood. He said, "Here is a man who likes a good joke." He told Robin Hood who he really was. Robin Hood was not mad. He laughed and laughed. The king invited Robin Hood to come and live in the castle. The castle was 20 miles away. Robin had to walk south, cross a river, and make two left turns to get there. He stayed inside the castle grounds for a year and a day.

Then, Robin grew restless and asked the king for permission to leave. The king did not want him to go. He said Robin Hood could visit Sherwood Forest for only one week. Robin said he missed his men but promised to return. The king knew Robin Hood never broke his promises.

Directions: Answer these questions about Robin Hood and the king.

1. Why do you think Robin Hood laughed when the king told him the truth?

   _____

2. Give directions from Sherwood Forest to the king's castle.

   _____

   _____

   _____

3. Circle the main idea:

   The king liked Robin Hood, but Robin missed his life in Sherwood Forest.

   Robin Hood thought the castle was boring.

Benjamin Franklin was born in Boston, Massachusetts, on January 17, 1706. Even though he only attended school to age 10, he worked hard to improve his mind and character. He taught himself several foreign languages and learned many skills that would later be a great help to him.

Benjamin Franklin played a very important part in our history. One of his many accomplishments was as a printer. He was a helper (apprentice) to his half-brother, James, and later moved to the city of Philadelphia where he worked in another print shop.

Another skill that he developed was writing. He wrote and published *Poor Richard's Almanac* in December 1732. Franklin was also a diplomat. He served our country in many ways, both in the United States and in Europe. As an inventor, he experimented with electricity. Have you heard about the kite and key experiment? Benjamin Franklin was able to prove that lightning has an electrical discharge.

Directions: Answer these questions about Benjamin Franklin.

1. Circle the main idea:

    Benjamin Franklin was a very important part of our history.

    Benjamin Franklin wrote *Poor Richard's Almanac*.

2. Write three of Benjamin Franklin's accomplishments.

    1) _____

    2) _____

    3) _____

Following Directions: Grow a Pineapple Plant

You can grow a pineapple plant at home. Here's how: Have a grown-up use a large sharp knife to slice off the very top of a pineapple. Fill a five-inch round pot with potting soil. Put the top of the pineapple in the soil.

Do not bury the plant too deep. Let most of the top show. Do not give your plant too much water! Pour on a little water when you plant it. Then, wait until the soil feels dry to water it again. Soon, it will grow roots.

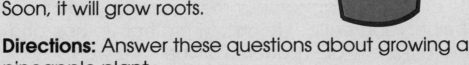

Directions: Answer these questions about growing a pineapple plant.

1. Where can you get potting soil?

   _____

   _____

2. What is the first step for growing a pineapple plant?

   _____

   _____

3. What is the second step?

   _____

   _____

4. Be careful about these two things when growing pineapple plants.

   1) Do not _____.

   2) Do not _____.

Have you ever seen morning glories? They begin to bloom in mid-May. Morning glory flowers grow on vines. They trail over the ground. Sometimes, the vines twine over other plants. They will grow over walls and fences. The vines on morning glory plants can grow to be 10 feet long! Morning glory flowers are bell-shaped. The flowers are white, pink, or blue. There are more than 200 different kinds of morning glory flowers!

Directions: Answer these questions about morning glories.

1. When do morning glories begin to bloom?

   _____

2. Morning glories grow on

   stems.

   vines.

3. What shape are morning glory flowers?

   _____

4. How many different kinds of morning glory flowers are there?

   _____

Directions: Reread the story about morning glories. Then, solve the puzzle.

Across:

1. Morning glories grow on these.

5. Morning glories sometimes twine over these.

6. Morning glories trail over this

Down:

2. Morning glory flowers are bell-_____.

3. Morning glory flowers can be pink, blue, or _____.

4. This is what morning glories do in mid-May.

Every living thing needs food. Did you ever wonder how plants get food? They do not sit down and eat a bowl of soup! Plants get their food from the soil and from water. To see how, cut off some stalks of celery. Put the stalks in a clear glass. Fill the glass half full of water. Add a few drops of red food coloring to the water. Leave it overnight. The next day, you will see that parts of the celery have turned red! The red lines show how the celery sucked up the water.

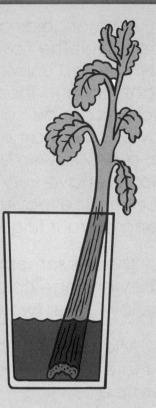

Directions: Answer these questions about how plants get food.

1. Name two ways plants get food.

    1) _____

    2) _____

2. Complete the four steps for using celery to see how plants get food.

    1) Cut off some stalks of _____.

    2) Put the stalks in _____.

    3) Fill the glass _____.

    4) Add a few drops of _____.

3. What do the red lines in the celery show?

    _____

    _____

Making Inferences: Fig Marigolds

Fig marigolds are beautiful! The flowers stay closed unless the light is bright. These flowers are also called by another name—the *mid-day flower*. Mid-day flowers have very long leaves. The leaves are as long as your finger!

There is something else unusual about mid-day flowers. They change color. When the flowers bloom, they are light yellow. After two or three days, they turn pink.

Mid-day flowers grow in California and South America where it is hot. They do not grow in other parts of the United States.

Directions: Answer these questions about fig marigolds.

1. Why do you think fig marigolds are also called mid-day flowers?

   _____

   _____

2. How long are the leaves of the mid-day flower?

   _____

   _____

3. Why do you think mid-day flowers do not grow all over the United States?

   _____

   _____

The soil in rainforests is very dark and rich. The trees and plants that grow there are very green. People who have seen one say a rainforest is "the greenest place on Earth." Why? Because it rains a lot. With so much rain, the plants stay very green. The ground stays very wet. Rainforests cover only 6 percent of Earth. But they are home to 66 percent of all the different kinds of plants and animals on Earth! Today, rainforests are threatened by such things as acid rain from factory smoke emissions around the world, and from farm expansion. Farmers living near rainforests cut down many trees each year to clear the land for farming. I wish I could see a rainforest. Do you?

Directions: Answer these questions about rainforests.

1. What do the plants and trees in a rainforest look like?

   _____

2. What is the soil like in a rainforest?

   _____

3. How much of Earth is covered by rainforests?

   _____

4. What percentage of Earth's plants and animals live there?

   _____

Comprehension: The Rainforest Lizard

Many strange animals live in the rainforest. One kind of strange animal is a very large lizard. This lizard grows as large as a dog! It has scales on its skin. It has a very wide mouth. It has spikes sticking out of the top of its head. It looks scary, but don't be afraid! This lizard eats mostly weeds. This lizard does not look very tasty, but other animals think it tastes good. Snakes eat these lizards. So do certain birds. Some people in the rainforest eat them, too! Would you like to eat a lizard for lunch?

Directions: Answer these questions about the rainforest lizard.

1. What is the size of this rainforest lizard?

   _____

2. Where do its scales grow?

   _____

3. Which kind of food does the lizard eat?

   _____

4. Who likes to eat these lizards?

   _____

The sloth spends most of its life in the trees of the rainforest. The three-toed sloth, for example, is usually hanging around, using its claws to keep it there. Because it is in the trees so much, it has trouble moving on the ground. Certainly it could be caught easily by other animals of the rainforest if it was being chased. The sloth is a very slow-moving animal.

Do you have any idea what the sloth eats? The sloth eats mostly leaves it finds in the treetops.

Have you ever seen a three- or two-toed sloth? If you see one in a zoo, you don't have to get close enough to count the toes. You can tell these two cousins apart in a different way—the three-toed sloth has some green mixed in with its fur because of the algae It gets from the trees.

Directions: Answer these questions about the sloth.

1. How does the three-toed sloth hang around the rainforest?

    a. by its tail, like a monkey

    b. by its claws, or toes

2. The main diet of the sloth is _It eats mostly leaves._

3. Why does the sloth have trouble moving around on the ground?

    because It could be caught
    easily by other animals if it benn chrsed

If you have ever seen a raccoon holding its food by its hands and carefully eating it, you would have an idea of how the kinkajou (king-kuh-joo) eats. This animal of the rainforest is a cousin of the raccoon. Unlike its North American cousin, though, it is a golden-brown color.

The kinkajou's head and body are 17 to 22 inches long. The long tail of the kinkajou comes in handy for hanging around its neighborhood! If you do some quick mental math you can get a good idea of its size. It weighs very little—about five pounds. (You may have a five-pound bag of sugar or flour in your kitchen to help you get an idea of the kinkajou's weight.)

This rainforest animal eats a variety of things. It enjoys nectar from the many rainforest flowers, insects, fruit, honey, birds, and other small animals. Because it lives mostly in the trees, the kinkajou has a ready supply of food.

Directions: Answer these questions about the kinkajou.

1. The kinkajou is a cousin to the _____.

2. Write three things the kinkajou eats.

    1) _____

    2) _____

    3) _____

Comprehension: The Jaguar

The jaguar weighs between 100 and 250 pounds. It can be as long as six feet! This is not your ordinary house cat!

One strange feature of the jaguar is its living arrangements. The jaguar has its own territory. No other jaguar lives in its home range. It would be very unusual for one jaguar to meet another in the rainforest. One way they mark their territory is by scratching trees.

Have you ever seen your pet cat hide in the grass and carefully and quietly sneak up on an unsuspecting grasshopper or mouse? Like its gentler, smaller cousin, the jaguar stalks its prey in the high grass. It likes to eat small animals, such as rodents, but can attack and kill larger animals such as tapirs, deer, and cattle. It is good at catching fish as well.

Directions: Answer these questions about the jaguar.

1. The jaguar lives:

    a. in large groups

    b. alone

    c. under water

2. This large cat marks its territory by:

    a. black marker

    b. roaring

    c. scratching trees

3. How much does it weigh?

_____

One interesting bird of the rainforest is the toucan. This bird has a very large bill which is shaped like a canoe. Sometimes, the toucan's bill can be as large as its body! The toucan's bill is colorful and hard, but flexible. You can also tell a toucan by its colorful feathers. They are mostly blue or black but also include red, yellow, and orange.

The heavy growth in the rainforest provides protective covering for this colorful bird. The toucan lives in the layer of the rainforest called the *canopy*. Here, high in the trees, it can use its large, hooked bill to find the berries and fruits that it loves to eat.

Directions: Answer these questions about the toucan.

1. Circle three characteristics of the toucan's bill.

    colorful   large

    brittle   pointed

    small   soft

2. In what layer of the rainforest does the toucan live?

    _____

3. What does the toucan love to eat?

    1) _____

    2) _____

4. What colors are the toucan's feathers?

    _____

Many people travel to the rainforest each year. Some go by car, some go by train, and some go by school bus! You don't even need a passport—the only thing you need is a field-trip permission slip.

If you live in the Cleveland, Ohio, area, you might get to take a class trip to the rainforest there. It is next to the Cleveland Zoo. This rainforest is a building that contains all the sights, sounds, smells, and temperatures of the real rainforest. You will get to see many of the animals, big and small, that you could see if you went to Central or South America. The plants that grow there also grow in the rainforest. It is an interesting way to get an idea of what life is like in that part of the world!

Directions: Answer these questions about visiting the rainforest.

1. If you lived in northern Ohio, name three ways you could get to the rainforest.

   _____

2. In this rainforest, you can see _____ and _____ that are found in the real rainforest.

3. The real rainforest is located in both _____ and _____ .

Review

Directions: Use the words in the box to complete these sentences about the rainforest. All the words will not be used.

algae	ten	jaguar	canopy
six	toucan	rhino	sixty-six
Cleveland, Ohio	dog	spider	kinkajou

1. The rainforest covers _____ percent of Earth.

2. This animal lives alone in the rainforest. _____.

3. The three-toed sloth gets its green color from _____ found in trees.

4. The _____ is a cousin of the raccoon.

5. People can visit the rainforest in _____.

6. One large lizard here grows as large as a _____.

7. The _____ is a very colorful bird.

8. The toucan lives in the _____ layer of the rainforest.

You can grow many kinds of flowers in a garden. Here are the names of some—trumpet vine, pitcher plant, and bird-of-paradise. The flowers that grow on these plants form seeds. The seeds can be used to grow new plants. The bird-of-paradise looks as if it has wings! The pitcher plant is very strange. It eats insects! The trumpet vine grows very long. It trails around fences and other plants. These plants are very different. Together, they make a pretty flower garden.

Bird of Paradise

Directions: Answer these questions about unusual flowers.

1. What do you think a pitcher plant looks like?

   _____

2. What do you think a trumpet vine looks like?

   _____

3. Name two of the three plants that grow seeds in their flowers.

   1) _____

   2) _____

4. What can the seeds be used for?

   _____

Main Idea: Unusual Plants

Do you have a cat? Do you have catnip growing around your home? If you don't know, your cat probably does. Cats love the catnip plant and can be seen rolling around in it. Some cat toys have catnip inside them because cats love it so much.

People can enjoy catnip, too. Some people make catnip tea with the leaves of the plant. It is like the mint with which people make tea.

Another refreshing drink can be made with the berries of the sumac bush or tree. Native Americans would pick the red berries, crush them, and add water to make a thirst-quenching drink. The berries were sour, but they must have believed that the cool, tart drink was refreshing. Does this remind you of lemonade?

Directions: Answer these questions about unusual plants.

1. What is the main idea of the first two paragraphs above?

    _____

    _____

2. Write two ways cats show that they love catnip.

    1) _____

    2) _____

3. How can people use catnip?

    _____

Comprehension: Dangerous Plants

You may have been warned about some plants. Poison ivy and poison oak are plants we usually learn about at an early age. The itching and burning some people get from touching or even being around these plants is enough to make  them extra careful. Have you ever walked through a field and felt like you had been stung? You probably touched the stinging nettle. This plant with jagged edges is a good one to avoid, too.

Other plants can be more dangerous. You should not pick and eat any berries, seeds, or nuts without first checking to make sure they are safe. You could get very sick or even die if you ate from one of these poisonous plants. Rhubarb and cherries are two common pie-making ingredients, but never eat the leaves of the rhubarb plant. The cherry leaves and branches have poison in them.

Directions: Answer these questions about dangerous plants.

1. You should not pick and eat any _____,

   _____, or _____ without first making sure they are safe.

2. _____ and _____ might make your skin itch and burn.

3. What would happen if you touched a stinging nettle plant?

   _____

   _____

Have you ever traveled through Arizona or other southwestern states of the United States? One type of plant you may have seen is the cactus. This plant and other desert thickets are homes to the cactus wren, the state bird of Arizona. It is interesting how this bird (which is the size of a robin) can roost on this **prickly** plant and keep from getting stuck on the sharp spines. The cactus wren builds its nest on top of these thorny desert plants.

The cactus wren's song is not a beautiful, musical sound. Instead, it is compared to the grating sound of machinery. You can also identify the bird by its coloring. It has white spots on its outer tail feathers and white eyebrows. The crown (head) of the cactus wren is a rusty color.

Directions: Answer these questions about the cactus wren.

1. In what part of the United States would you find the cactus wren?

   _____

2. What does **prickly** mean?

   a. soft   b. green   c. having sharp points

3. Do you think you would like to hear the song of the cactus wren? Why or why not?

   _____

   _____

   _____

Along the sandy coastline of Louisiana you may see the brown pelican. It is not hard to identify this large bird with a throat pouch. When it is young, the brown pelican has a dark-brown body and head. If you see this bird with a brown body and a white head, you are looking at an adult.

Do you know what the brown pelican uses its large throat pouch for? If you said the pouch is used for carrying the fish it catches, you would be wrong. Many people think that is how the pouch is used, but the pouch is really used for separating the fish from the water. Just imagine how much water the brown pelican can scoop up as it fishes!

Directions: Answer these questions about the brown pelican.

1. The brown pelican is found mostly along the

   _____ of Louisiana.

2. How does it catch its food?

   _____

   _____

3. How is a young pelican's coloring different from the adult pelican?

   _____

   _____

   _____

Comprehension: State Bird — Maine

The chickadee may visit your bird feeder on a regular basis if you live in Maine. This bird seems to have a feeding schedule so it doesn't miss a meal! The chickadee can be tamed to eat right out of your hand. If this bird sees some insect eggs on a tree limb, it will hang upside down to get at this treat.

The chickadee lives in forests and open woodlands throughout most of the year, but when winter comes, it moves into areas populated by people. It is colored gray with a black cap and white on its underside and cheeks.

The chickadee lives in the northern half of the United States and in southern and western Canada. The western part of Alaska is also home to this **curious** and tame little bird.

Directions: Answer these questions about the chickadee.

1. What does **curious** mean?

   a. underside   c. tame

   b. questioning   d. schedule

2. What does the chickadee do when winter comes?

   _____

   _____

3. One of the chickadee's favorite treats is

   _____.

The cardinal is the state bird of Ohio. You probably know that the cardinal is red, but do you know how this bright red bird (males are red; females are brown with some red) got its name? Its name came from the bright red robes of the Roman Catholic cardinals.

Cardinals live in gardens as well as brushy swamps, thickets, and the edges of woodlands. This bird can be found, year-round, in the eastern half of the United States. Some parts of southern California and Arizona are also home to this bird.

If you have a bird feeder, you have probably seen a cardinal there. Its main diet is seeds, but it also sometimes eats insects. The song of the cardinal can be heard throughout the year, so you don't have to wait for the warmer weather of spring.

Directions: Answer these questions about the cardinal.

1. Which paragraph tells you where the cardinal lives?

   a. paragraph 1   b. paragraph 2   c. paragraph 3

2. What do cardinals eat?

   _____

3. How did this bird get its name?

   _____

   _____

4. Which is red in color, the male or female cardinal?

   _____

Main Idea: Hawks

Hawks are birds of prey. They **prey upon** other birds and animals. This means they kill other animals and eat them. The hawk has long pointed wings. It uses them to soar through the air as it looks for prey. It looks at the ground while it soars.

When it sees an animal or bird to eat, the hawk swoops down. It grabs the animal in its beak and claws, then carries it off and eats it. The hawk eats birds, rats, ground squirrels, and other pests.

Directions: Answer these questions about hawks.

1. Circle the main idea:

   Hawks are mean because they swoop down from the sky and eat animals and birds.

   Hawks are helpful because they eat sick birds, rats, ground squirrels, and other pests.

2. What kind of wings does a hawk have?

   _____

3. How does the hawk pick up its prey?

   _____

   _____

4. What does **prey upon** mean?

   _____

What is instinct (in-stinkt)? Instinct is knowing how to do something without being told how. Animals have instincts. Birds have an amazing instinct. It is called the *homing instinct*. The homing instinct is birds' inner urge to find their way somewhere. When birds fly south in the winter, how do they know where to go? How do they know how to get there? When they return in the spring, what makes them return to the same place they left? It is birds' homing instinct. People do not have a homing instinct. That is why we get lost so often!

Directions: Answer these questions about birds' homing instinct.

1. What word means knowing how to do something without being told?

   _____

2. What is birds' inner urge to find their way somewhere called?

   _____

3. Which direction do birds fly in the winter?

   _____

4. Do people have a homing instinct?

   _____

5. When do birds return home?

   _____

Directions: Reread the story about birds' homing instinct. Then, solve the puzzle.

Across:

3. Knowing how to do something without being told

4. This is when birds return from the south.

6. They have no homing instinct, so people get _____.

Down:

1. Birds fly south at this time.

2. They have a homing instinct.

5. They do not have a homing instinct.

Did you know that some people keep crickets as pets? These people always keep two crickets together. That way, the crickets do not get lonely!

Crickets are kept in a flowerpot filled with dirt. The dirt helps the crickets feel at home. They are used to being outside. Over the flowerpot is a covering that lets air inside. It also keeps the crickets in! Some people use a small net; others use cheesecloth. They make sure there is room under the covering for crickets to hop!

Pet crickets like to eat bread and lettuce. They also like raw hamburger meat. Would you like to have a pet cricket?

Directions: Answer these questions about pet crickets.

1. Where do pet crickets live?

   They Live in a flowerpot.

2. Why should you put dirt in with the crickets?

   It helps them feel at home

3. What is placed over the flowerpot?

   a covering

4. Write three things pet crickets like to eat.

   1) _bread_

   2) _lettuce_

   3) _hamburger meat_

Comprehension: Crickets

Directions: Read more about crickets. Then, solve the puzzle.

Only the male cricket can sing. He sings by moving his right wing quickly over his left. It is sort of like playing a violin. The cricket's song is the first insect song we hear in the spring. It is the last insect song we hear in the fall. Crickets do not sing in the winter.

Across:

1. Crickets are a kind of _____.

4. The movements for making a cricket song are like playing a _____.

6. The cricket makes his song with his _____.

7. This cricket cannot sing.

Down:

2. The cricket's song is the first insect's song we hear in the _____.

3. Crickets do not sing during this season.

5. To sing, the cricket moves this wing over his left wing.

Directions: Read the silly poem about what animals say. Then, answer the questions.

Wouldn't it be strange?
Wouldn't you say "Wow!"
If the dog said "moo,"
And the cow said "bow-wow,"
And the cat flew and sang,
And the bird said "meow"?
Wouldn't it be strange?
Wouldn't you say "Wow"?

1. What strange things would the cat do?

   _____

2. What strange thing would the bird do?

   _____

3. What strange thing would the cow do?

   _____

4. What strange thing would the dog do?

   _____

A cactus is a plant that lives in a hot, dry place. More than one cactus are called *cacti*. You can find cacti in the desert. Cacti grow in the southwestern United States. Instead of leaves, most cacti have spines. The spines help to protect the cactus against animals that might want to eat it. The spines also provide shade and prevent the cactus from losing too much water. Have you ever seen a cactus?

Directions: Answer these questions about cacti.

1. What do you call more than one cactus?

   _____

2. Where can you find cacti?

   _____

3. How do spines help the cactus?

   _____

   _____

   _____

Heather is a beautiful word for a beautiful plant. Some girls are also named Heather. Heather grows high in the mountains of the western United States. It needs very wet ground in which to grow. In the high mountains, snow keeps the ground wet enough for heather. It may be as short as four inches high or as tall as 12 inches. The flowers that grow on heather are a light pinkish-red color. The flowers bloom in June, July, and August. Heather is a wildflower. It is one of about 250,000 flowering plants. Have you ever seen a heather plant?

Directions: Answer these questions about heather.

1. Where in the United States does heather grow?

_____

_____

2. Circle the main idea:

   Heather is a beautiful wildflower that grows in the mountains.

   Heather is one of 250,000 different kinds of flowering plants.

3. Complete these directions on where to find heather.

   1) Wait until these months to look for heather:

   _____

   2) Go to the high _____.

   3) Look for ground that is _____.

Comprehension: Our Solar System

There are eight planets in our solar system. All of them circle the Sun. The planet closest to the Sun is named Mercury. The Greeks said Mercury was the messenger of the gods. The second planet from the Sun is named Venus. Venus shines the brightest. Venus was the Greek goddess of beauty. Earth is the third planet from the Sun. It is about the same size as Venus. After Earth is Mars, which is named after the Greek god of war. The other four planets are Jupiter, Saturn, Uranus, and Neptune. They, too, are named after Greek gods.

Directions: Answer these questions about our solar system.

1. How many planets are in our solar system?

   There are eight planets in the

2. What do the planets circle?

   All of them circle the sun.

3. What are the planets named after?

   mars, Venus, Mercury Earth,

4. Which planet is closest to the Sun?

   mercury.

5. Which planet is about the same size as Earth?

   Venus.

6. Which planet comes after Earth in the solar system?

   After Earth is mars.

In 1974, for the first time, a U.S. spacecraft passed within 400 miles of the planet Mercury. The name of the spacecraft was *Mariner 10*. There were no people on the spacecraft, but there were cameras that could take clear pictures from a long distance. What the pictures showed was interesting. They showed that Mercury's surface was a lot like the surface of the Moon. The surface of Mercury is filled with huge holes called *craters*. A layer of fine dust covers Mercury. This, too, is like the dust on the Moon. There is no life on either Mercury or the Moon.

Directions: Answer these questions about Mercury.

1. What was the name of the spacecraft that went near Mercury?

   _____

2. What was on the spacecraft?

   _____

3. Write two ways that Mercury is like the Moon.

   1) _____

   2) _____

4. Is there life on Mercury?

   _____

Main Idea: Venus

For many years, no one knew much about Venus. When people looked through telescopes, they could not see past Venus' clouds. Long ago, people thought the clouds covered living things. Spacecraft radar has shown this is not true. Venus is too hot for life to exist. The temperature on Venus is about 900 degrees! Remember how hot you were the last time it was 90 degrees? Now, imagine it being 10 times hotter. Nothing could exist in that heat. It is also very dry on Venus. For life to exist, water must be present. Because of the heat and dryness, we know there are no people, plants, or other life on Venus.

Directions: Answer these questions about Venus.

1. Circle the main idea:

   We cannot see past Venus' clouds to know what the planet is like.

   Spacecraft radar shows it is too hot and dry for life to exist on Venus.

2. What is the temperature on Venus? _____

3. In the past, why did people think life might exist on Venus?

   _____

   _____

One planet in our solar system certainly supports life—Earth. Our planet is the third planet from the Sun and takes 365 days, or one year, to orbit the Sun. This rotation makes it possible for most of our planet to have four seasons—winter, spring, summer, and fall.

Besides being able to support life, our planet is unique in another way—Earth is 75 percent covered by water. No other planet has that much, if any, liquid on its surface. This liquid and its evaporation help provide the cloud cover and our climate patterns.

Earth has one natural satellite—the Moon. Scientists and other experts all over the world have created and sent into orbit other satellites used for a variety of purposes—communication, weather forecasting, and so on.

Directions: Answer these questions about Earth.

1. How much of Earth is covered by water? _____

2. How long does it take Earth to orbit the Sun?

   _____

3. How does water make Earth the "living planet"?

   _____

   _____

   _____

The U.S. has sent many unmanned spacecrafts to Mars since 1964. (Unmanned means there were no people on the spacecraft.) That's why scientists know a lot about this planet. Mars has low temperatures. There is no water on Mars. There is only a gas called *water vapor*. There is also ice on Mars. Scientists have also learned that there is

fog on Mars in the early morning! Do you remember when you last saw fog here on Earth? Scientists say the fog on Mars looks the same. As on Earth, the fog occurs in low-lying areas of the ground.

Another interesting thing about Mars is that it is very windy. The wind blows up many dust storms on this planet. A spacecraft called *Mariner* 9 was the first to take pictures of dust storms. Later, the unmanned *Viking* spacecraft landed on the surface of Mars.

Directions: Answer these questions about Mars.

1. On Mars, it is

   cold.   hot.

2. When there are no people on a spacecraft, it is

   _____.

3. These are caused by all the wind on Mars.

   _____

4. This spacecraft took pictures of dust storms on Mars.

   _____

Directions: Reread the story about Mars. Then, solve the puzzle.

Across:

1. This spacecraft landed on the surface of Mars.

3. This travels through the solar system.

5. Is it hot on Mars?

6. The wind on Mars blows up dust _____.

Down:

1. There is no water on Mars. There is water _____.

2. This spacecraft took the first pictures of Mars' dust storms.

4. This occurs on Earth and Mars in the early morning.

Jupiter, the fifth planet from the Sun, is circled by a ring of dark particles. It takes this planet almost 12 years to orbit the Sun. Jupiter's ring is very difficult to see from Earth without using special equipment. Jupiter is the largest planet in our solar system. It is 11 times bigger than Earth!

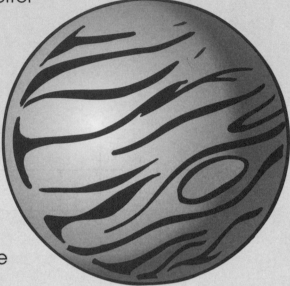

Scientists have been able to learn much about this planet because of the information received from *Voyager I* in 1979. They know that we cannot send a spacecraft to land on the surface of Jupiter as we have done with the Moon. The surface of Jupiter is not solid. The outer shell of Jupiter is gas.

Directions: Answer these questions about Jupiter.

1. In what year did *Voyager I* send us more information about Jupiter?

   _____

2. Why can't we send a spacecraft to land on Jupiter?

   _____

   _____

3. What is the largest planet in our solar system?

   _____

4. Jupiter is the _____ planet from the Sun.

Have you looked at Saturn through a strong telescope? If you have, you know it has rings. Saturn is the most beautiful planet to see! It is bright yellow. It is circled by four rings. Two bright rings are on the outside of the circle. Two dark rings are on the inside. The rings of Saturn are made of billions of tiny bits of rocks. The rocks travel around the planet in a swarm. They keep their ring shape as the planet travels around the Sun. These rings shine brightly, and so does the planet Saturn. Both reflect the rays of the Sun. The Sun is 885 million miles away from Saturn. It takes Saturn $29\frac{1}{2}$ years to travel around the Sun!

Directions: Answer these questions about Saturn.

1. How many rings does Saturn have? _____

2. What are Saturn's rings made of?

   _____

3. What causes Saturn and its rings to shine?

   _____

4. How far away from the Sun is Saturn?

   _____

William Herschel discovered the planet Uranus in 1781. As has happened many times throughout history with other scientists, inventors, and explorers, he didn't realize he had found a planet—he thought it was a comet. Scientists didn't know too much about this planet, though, until 1986 when the U.S. spacecraft *Voyager 2* flew past it.

Do you think the planet Earth is big? Well, the planet Uranus is four times bigger! Uranus is another planet that has rings. While Saturn's rings are made of ice, the rings of Uranus are made of dark particles the size of boulders. Earth has one natural satellite—the Moon—but Uranus has 15 natural satellites. It takes Earth one year to circle the Sun, but Uranus takes 84 years! Uranus is the seventh planet from the Sun.

Directions: Answer these questions about Uranus.

1. This story tells about two planets that have rings. They are:

   1) _____   2) _____

2. Who was William Herschel?

   _____

3. Which planet is bigger, Earth or Uranus? How much bigger?

   _____

Neptune is the eighth planet from the Sun. Because of its location, it takes Neptune 168 years to orbit the Sun. It is closely related to Uranus, one of its neighbors in the solar system. Scientists have noticed that its coloring and appearance look very similar to that of Uranus.

Neptune was discovered by Galle in 1846. It is almost four times bigger than Earth. Neptune has two known satellites—the larger is named *Triton* and the smaller is named *Nereid*. Some scientists have noticed that the orbit of the larger satellite is getting closer and closer to the planet. It will eventually crash into the surface of Neptune. However, you and I won't be able to watch this happen. Scientists predict it will happen in 100 million years!

Directions: Answer these questions about Neptune.

1. Why does it take Neptune 168 years to orbit the Sun?

   _____

2. What are the names of Neptune's two satellites?

   1) _____   2) _____

3. Which word in the last paragraph means *to tell about something that will happen*?

   _____

4. Who discovered the planet Neptune?

   _____

Constellations are groups of stars that have been given names. They often represent an animal, person, or object. One of the easiest constellations to identify is the Big Dipper, which is shaped like a spoon. Once the Big Dipper is located, it is easy to see Cassiopeia (a W), the Little Dipper (an upside-down spoon), and the North Star. The North Star's scientific name is **Polaris**, and it is the last star in the handle of the Little Dipper. Other constellations include Orion the hunter, Gemini the twins, Canis Major the dog, and Pegasus the winged horse.

The Constellation Orion

Directions: Answer these questions about constellations.

1. What are **constellations**?

   _____

2. Why is the Big Dipper easy to identify?

   _____

3. What is the Little Dipper shaped like?

   _____

4. What is **Polaris**?

   _____

Our moon is not the only moon in the solar system. Some other planets have moons also. Saturn has 10 moons! Our moon is Earth's closest neighbor in the solar system. Sometimes, our moon is 225,727 miles away. Other times, it is 252,002 miles away. Why? Because the Moon revolves around Earth. It does not go around Earth in a perfect circle. So, sometimes its path takes it further away from our planet.

When our astronauts visited the Moon, they found dusty plains, high mountains, and huge craters. There is no air or water on the Moon. That is why life cannot exist there. The astronauts had to wear space suits to protect their skin from the bright Sun. They had to take their own air to breathe. They had to take their own food and water. The Moon was an interesting place to visit. Would you want to live there?

Directions: Answer these questions about the Moon.

1. Circle the main idea:

   The Moon travels around Earth, and the astronauts visited the Moon.

   Astronauts found that the Moon—Earth's closest neighbor—has no air or water and cannot support life.

2. Make a list of what to take on a trip to the Moon.

   _____

   _____

   _____

   _____

Recalling Details: Your Amazing Body

Directions: Read about the human body. Then, solve the puzzle.

Your body is like an amazing machine. Every minute, your heart pumps six quarts of blood. Your brain sends thousands of messages to other parts of your body. The messages travel along the nerves at more than 100 miles an hour! Your lungs fill with air. Your ears hear sounds. Your eyes see pictures. And you thought you were just sitting here reading! Your body is always very busy, even when you sleep.

Across:

2. Your body is an amazing _____.

4. Even when you sleep, your body is always _____.

5. You hear with these.

6. This is what you hear.

Down:

1. Your eyes see these.

2. Your brain sends thousands of these to other parts of the body.

3. These fill with air.

Make your hand into a fist. Now look at it. That is about the size of your heart! Your heart is a strong pump. It works all the time. Right now, it is beating about 90 times a minute. When you run, it beats about 150 times a minute.

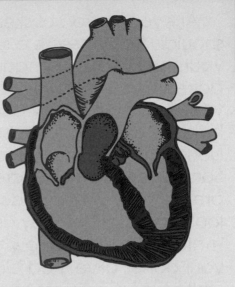

Inside, your heart has four spaces. The two spaces on the top are called *atria*. This is where blood is pumped into the heart. The two spaces on the bottom are called *ventricles*. This is where blood is pumped out of the heart. The blood is pumped to every part of your body. How? Open and close your fist. See how it tightens and loosens? The heart muscle tightens and loosens, too. This is how it pumps blood.

Directions: Answer these questions about your heart.

1. How often does your heart work?

   _____

2. How fast does it beat when you are sitting?

   _____

3. How fast does it beat when you are running?

   _____

4. How many spaces are inside your heart?

   _____

Making Inferences: Your Bones

Are you scared of skeletons? You shouldn't be. There is a skeleton inside of you! The skeleton is made up of all the bones in your body. These 206 bones give you your shape. They also protect your heart and everything else inside. Your bones come in many sizes. Some are short. Some are long. Some are rounded. Some are very tiny. The outside of your bones looks solid. Inside, they are filled with a soft material called *marrow*. This is what keeps your bones alive. Red blood cells and most white blood cells are made here. These cells help feed the body and fight disease.

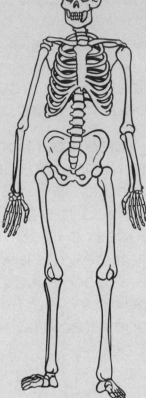

Directions: Answer these questions about your bones.

1. Do you think your leg bone is short, long, or rounded?

   _____

2. Do you think the bones in your head are short, long, or rounded?

   _____

3. What is something soft inside your bones?

   _____

4. How many bones are in your skeleton?

   _____

Can you make a fist? You could not do this without muscles. You need muscles to make your body move. You have muscles everywhere. There are muscles in your legs. There are even muscles in your tongue!

Remember, your heart is a muscle. It is called an **involuntary muscle** because it works without help from you. Your stomach muscles are also involuntary. You don't need to tell your stomach to digest food. Other muscles are called **voluntary muscles**. You must tell these muscles to move. Most voluntary muscles are hooked to bones. When the muscles squeeze, they cause the bone to move. Without your muscles, you would be nothing but a bag of bones!

Directions: Answer these questions about your muscles.

1. What are **involuntary muscles**?

   _____

2. What are **voluntary muscles**?

   _____

3. What causes bones to move?

   _____

Directions: Read more about your muscles. Then, solve the puzzle.

Did you know your muscles have names? Their names have to do with the jobs they perform. The muscles that pull your forearms down are called *triceps*. **Tri** means *three*. The triceps have three parts of muscle working together. The muscles that pull your forearms up are called *biceps*. **Bi** means *two*. The biceps have two parts of muscle working together. Each set of muscles has a certain job to do. Muscles in the front of the foot pull your toes up. Muscles on the back of the thighs bend your knees. Aren't you glad you have muscles?

Across:

2. Each set of muscles has a certain _____ to do.

4. These muscles pull your forearms down.

5. Muscles on the back of the thighs bend these.

Down:

1. Without these, you would be a bag of bones.

3. These muscles pull your forearms up.

4. Muscles on the front of your foot pull these up.

Wiggle your fingers. Now, clap your hands. That was easy, wasn't it? But it wasn't as easy as you think! Each of your hands has 27 bones. Eight of the 27 bones are in your wrist. There are five bones in each of your palms. Your hands have many muscles, too. It takes 30 muscles to wiggle your fingers. When you use your hands, the bones and muscles work together. Remember this the next time you cut your meat. You will use your wrist bones and muscles. You will use your finger bones and muscles. Cutting your meat seems easy. It is—thanks to your muscles and bones!

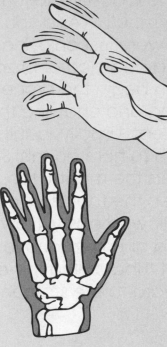

Directions: Answer these questions about your hands.

1. How many bones are in each of your wrists?

   _____

2. How many bones are in each of your hands?

   _____

3. How many bones are in each of your palms?

   _____

4. Add together the palm bones and wrist bones. Subtract from the total number of bones in the hand. How many bones are left?

   _____

The digestive system begins in your mouth. (And you thought you were just enjoying that salad and slice of pizza!) The teeth begin the process by slicing and chewing the food you eat. Usually, adults have 32 teeth to help do this. Saliva enters the mouth, too, and helps soften the food so it can be swallowed easily. Now, your salad and pizza move through a short tube called the *esophagus* onward to the stomach.

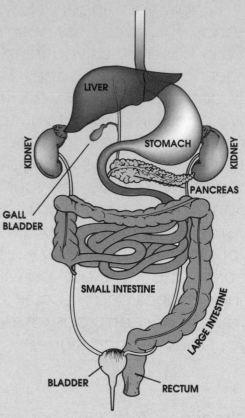

LIVER

KIDNEY

STOMACH

KIDNEY

PANCREAS

GALL BLADDER

SMALL INTESTINE

LARGE INTESTINE

BLADDER

RECTUM

Directions: Answer these questions about your digestive system.

1. What does saliva do?

   _____

   _____

2. Where does the digestive system begin?

   _____

3. What do your teeth do?

   _____

4. The _____ is a short tube that brings food to the stomach.

It's here in the stomach that food is stored long enough to let it mix with six pints of gastric juices. These important juices help kill bacteria and break down food into nutrients that your body needs.

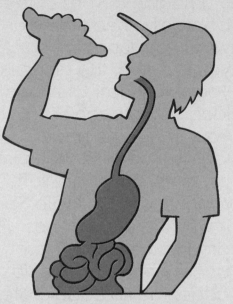

Next, the food moves into the small intestine. This section of the digestive system helps to continue breaking down the food into nutrients needed by your body. From here, most of the nutrients needed are absorbed.

The final stage of the digestive system takes place in the large intestine, or colon. The colon helps send into the body any leftover usable products, water, and salt.

Directions: Answer these questions about your digestive system.

1. How do the gastric juices help digestion?

_____

What is their function?

_____

2. Where does the final stage of digestion take place?

_____

3. Number the order of where digestion takes place.

_____ large intestine   _____ mouth

_____ esophagus   _____ small intestine

_____ stomach

Main Idea: Your Lungs

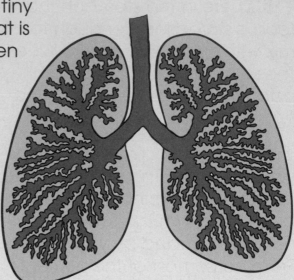

Imagine millions of teeny, tiny balloons joined together. That is what your lungs are like. When you breathe, the air goes to your two lungs. One lung is located on each side of your chest. The heart is located between the two lungs. The lungs are soft, spongy, and delicate. That is why there are bones around the lungs. These bones are called the *rib cage*. The rib cage protects the lungs so they can do their job. The lungs bring oxygen (ox-i-gin) into the body. They also take waste out of the body. This waste is called *carbon dioxide*. We could not live without our lungs!

Directions: Answer these questions about your lungs.

1. Circle the main idea:

   The lungs are spongy and located in the chest. They are like small balloons.

   The lungs bring in oxygen and take out carbon dioxide. We could not live without our lungs.

2. What is the name of the bones around your lungs?

   _____

3. What is located between the lungs?

   _____

4. What goes into your lungs when you breathe?

   _____

Do you know how people traveled before cars? They rode horses! Often, the horses were hooked up to wagons. Some horses were hooked up to carriages. Wagons were used to carry supplies. Carriages had covered tops. They were used to carry people. Both wagons and carriages were pulled by horses.

The first cars in the United States were invented shortly before the year 1900. These cars looked a lot like carriages. The seats were high off the ground. They had very thin wheels. The difference was that they were powered by engines. Carriages were pulled by horses. Still, they looked alike. People called the first cars *horseless carriages*.

Directions: Answer these questions about horseless carriages.

1. Write one way wagons and carriages were the same.

   _____

2. When were the first cars invented?

   _____

3. Why were the first cars called *horseless carriages*?

   _____

   _____

Comprehension: Horseless Carriage

Directions: Read more about the first cars. Then, solve the puzzle.

Can you guess how many cars there were in the United States about 100 years ago? Only four! Today, nearly every family has a car. Most families have two cars. Henry Ford started the Ford Motor Company in 1903. His first car was called the *Model T.* People thought cars would never be used in place of horses. Ford had to sell his cars through department stores! Soon, cars became popular. By 1920, there were 200 different U.S. companies making cars!

Across:

2. _____ Ford began making cars in 1903.

4. At first, cars were sold in department _____.

5. By 1920, there were 200 different companies making these.

Down:

1. Henry Ford's first car was called a _____.

2. At first, people thought cars would never replace _____.

3. Ford's company was called the Ford _____ Company.

A snowblower is used to blow snow off sidewalks and driveways. It is faster than using a shovel. It is also easier! Airports use snowblowers, too. They use them to clear the runways that planes use. Many airports use a giant snowblower. It is a type of truck. This snowblower weighs 30,000 pounds! It can blow 100,000 pounds of snow every minute. It cuts through the snow with huge blades. The blades are over six feet tall.

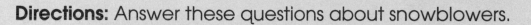

Directions: Answer these questions about snowblowers.

1. Why do people use snowblowers instead of shovels?

   _____

2. What do airports use snowblowers for?

   _____

3. How much do some airport snowblowers weigh?

   _____

4. How much snow can the airport snowblower blow every minute?

   _____

5. What does the snowblower use to cut through snow?

   _____

What would we do without trucks? Your family may not own a truck, but everyone depends on trucks. Trucks bring our food to stores. Trucks deliver our furniture. Trucks carry new clothes to shopping centers. The goods of the world move on trucks.

Trucks are harder to make than cars. They must be sturdy. They carry heavy loads. They cannot break down.

The first trucks were on the road in 1900. Like trains, they were powered by steam engines. They did not use gasoline. The first trucks did not have heavy wheels. Their engines often broke down.

Trucks changed when the U.S. entered World War I in 1917. Big, heavy tires were put on trucks. Gasoline engines were used. Trucks used in war had to be sturdy. Lives were at stake!

Directions: Answer these questions about the first trucks.

1. What powered the first trucks?

   _____

2. When did early trucks begin using gasoline engines?

   _____

3. How do trucks serve us?

   _____

   _____

Trains have been around much longer than cars or trucks. The first train used in the United States was made in England. It was brought to the U.S. in 1829. Because it was light green, it was nicknamed the *Grasshopper*. Unlike a real grasshopper, this train was not fast. It only went 10 miles an hour.

That same year, another train was built by an American. Compared to the *Grasshopper*, the American train was fast. It went 30 miles an hour. People were amazed. This train was called the *Rocket*. Can you guess why?

Directions: Answer these questions about the first trains.

1. Where was the first train made that was used in the U.S.?

   The First train was made in England

2. What did people call this train?

   The People call This Train The Grasshopper

3. What year did the *Grasshopper* arrive in the U.S.?

   It arrived in The U.S. in 1829.

4. What American train was built that same year?

   The Train was called The Rocket.

Comprehension: The First Trains

Directions: Reread the story of the first trains. Read the clues and fill in the blanks with your answers. Then, circle your answers in the word search.

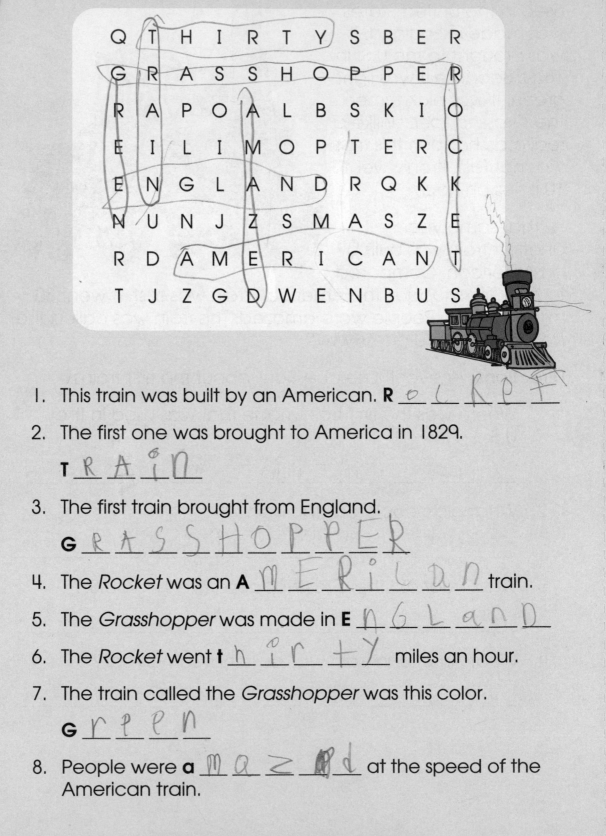

```
Q T H I R T Y S B E R
G R A S S H O P P E R
R A P O A L B S K I O
E I L I M O P T E R C
E N G L A N D R Q K K
N U N J Z S M A S Z E
R D A M E R I C A N T
T J Z G D W E N B U S
```

1. This train was built by an American. **R** _o l k e t_

2. The first one was brought to America in 1829.

   T _R A I n_

3. The first train brought from England.

   G _R A S S H O P P E R_

4. The *Rocket* was an **A** _M E R I L a n_ train.

5. The *Grasshopper* was made in **E** _n G L a n D_

6. The *Rocket* went t _h i r t y_ miles an hour.

7. The train called the *Grasshopper* was this color.

   G _r e e n_

8. People were a _m a z e d_ at the speed of the American train.

Trains are noisy! It is hard to hear around trains. That is why hand signals are used. The signals tell the engineer who drives the train many things. There is a signal to tell him or her to stop completely. Another signal tells him or her to reduce speed. Other signals tell the engineer to proceed, apply brakes, release brakes, and back up. These six signals are very important.

During daylight, the signals are made with a white or red kerchief. At night, the signals are made with a big lantern that can be easily seen. A signal man moves the lantern. The arrows in the pictures show which way the lantern is moved.

| stop | reduce speed | apply brakes | release brakes | back up | proceed |

Directions: Answer these questions about hand signals for trains.

1. Why is a lantern used for hand signals at night?

   Because it can be easily seen.

2. Who drives the train?

   The engineer.

3. Look at the pictures. Give directions for signaling the engineer to stop.

   _____

   _____

Comprehension: Beavers

Have you ever been called a busy beaver? You may not know what this expression means, but read the paragraphs below to find out.

Most animals cannot change where they live. A bird can build a nest and a mole can burrow into the ground, but the beaver can do more than that. If it likes a certain area but finds that the water is not deep enough, do you know what it can do? The beaver gets busy and starts cutting down trees to build a dam so that the area covered by water is deeper and larger.

The beaver does this using its sharp teeth. After it gnaws on a tree, it cuts away until the tree starts to fall. The beaver makes sure to get out of the way! It then trims off the branches and bark. Without using a chainsaw, as a person would do, the beaver cuts the wood into smaller pieces.

Directions: Answer these questions about the beaver.

1. What does the beaver use to chop down a tree?

   _____

2. After the tree has fallen, what does the beaver do?

   _____

3. How did the term busy beaver come about?

   _____

   _____

   _____

The beaver is not only a great lumberjack, it can also swim quite well. Its special fur helps to keep it warm; its hind legs work like fins; its tail is used as a rudder to steer it through the water. The beaver can hold its breath under water for 15 minutes, and its special eyelids are transparent, so they work like goggles!

Even though the beaver is a very good swimmer and can stay under water for a long time, it does not live under water. When the beaver builds a dam, it also builds a lodge. A lodge is a dome-shaped structure above water level in which the beaver lives. The beaver enters its lodge through underwater tunnels. The lodge provides a place for the beaver to rest, eat, and raise young.

Directions: Answer these questions about the beaver.

1. What is the main idea of the first paragraph?

   _____

   _____

2. Which word in the first paragraph means *able to see through*?

   _____

3. How long can the beaver hold its breath under water?

   _____

Comprehension: Cows

Thousands of years ago, people domesticated (tamed) cows. If you live on or near a farm, you may see cows every day. You may know what it is like to hear their mooing sounds when they are ready to be fed or milked.

Cows are raised for meat and milk. If a cow is raised for the sole purpose of providing milk, it is called a *dairy cow*. Some common breeds of dairy cows are Holstein-Friesians (hole-steen free-zhunz), Jerseys, Brown Swiss, and Guernseys (gurn-zeez). Cows raised for their meat are Herefords (her-ferdz).

Cows use their long tails to swat flies and other bothersome bugs. Cows chew cud. This is a portion of their food that has already been chewed a little. It is swallowed, then brought back up after it has been combined with liquid. The cow has four stomachs which make this possible. What do you think of chewing cud? Yuck!

Directions: Answer these questions about cows.

1. Holstein-Friesians and Guernseys are two kinds of

   _____ cows.

2. Cows have _____ stomachs.

3. Another word for tamed is _____.

4. A common breed of cow raised for meat is

   _____.

Making Inferences: Sheep

Sheep like to stay close together. They do not run off. They move together in a flock. They live on sheep ranches. Some sheep grow 20 pounds of fleece each year. After it is cut off, the fleece is called *wool*. Cutting off the wool is called *shearing*. It does not hurt the sheep to be sheared. The wool is very warm and is used to make clothing.

Female sheep are called *ewes* ("yous"). Some types of ewes have only one baby each year. The baby is called a *lamb*. Other types of ewes have two or three lambs each year.

Directions: Answer these questions about sheep.

1. Why is sheep's behavior helpful to sheep ranchers?

   _____

2. If you were a sheep farmer, would you rather own the kind of sheep that has one baby each year, or one that has two or three?

   _____

   Why?

   _____

3. When it is still on the sheep, what is wool called?

   _____

Making Inferences: Sheep

Farmers shear sheep at the time of the year when the climate is warm. Shearing is usually done in May in the northern states and as early as February or March in the warmer southern states.

Whether in a small or large flock, sheep must be watched more carefully than cattle. Herders take care of sheep on the open range. The herders live in tents, campers, or camp wagons and take care of 500–2,000 sheep. As the sheep get larger, the herder must make sure that there is plenty of grass for the herd to **graze**.

Directions: Answer these questions about sheep.

1. What does **graze** mean?

    run   eat   like

2. Why do you think shearing takes place when the climate is warm?

    _____

    _____

3. What do think an open range is?

    _____

    _____

Rhinos are the second largest land animal. Only elephants are bigger.

Most people think rhinos are ugly. Their full name is rhinoceros (rhy-nos-ur-us). There are five kinds of rhinos—the square-lipped rhino, black rhino, great Indian rhino, Sumatran (sue-ma-trahn) rhino, and Javan rhino.

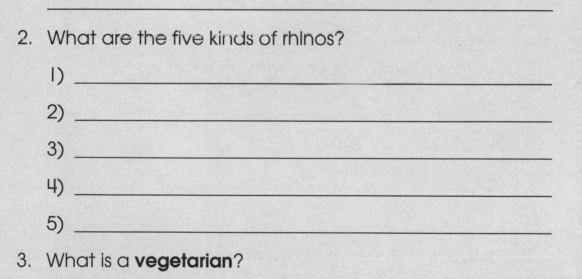

Rhinos have a great sense of smell, which helps protect them. They can smell other animals far away. They don't eat them, though. Rhinos do not eat meat. They are **vegetarians**.

Directions: Answer these questions about rhinos.

1. What is the largest land animal?

   _____

2. What are the five kinds of rhinos?

   1) _____

   2) _____

   3) _____

   4) _____

   5) _____

3. What is a **vegetarian**?

   _____

   _____

Have you ever heard this old song? "Oh, the red, red robin goes bob-bob-bobbin' along!" It's hard not to smile when you see a robin. Robins were first called *redbreasts*. If you have seen one, you know why! The fronts of their bodies are red. Robins are cheerful-looking birds.

Robins sing a sweet, mellow song. That is another reason why people like robins. The female robin lays two to six eggs. She sits on them for two weeks. Then, the father and mother robin both bring food to the baby birds. Robins eat spiders, worms, insects, and small seeds. Robins will also eat food scraps people put out for them.

Directions: Answer these questions about robins.

1. Write one reason people like robins.

   _____

2. How many eggs does a mother robin lay?

   _____

3. What do robins eat?

   _____

   _____

4. Who sits on the robin's eggs?

   _____

Directions: Reread the story about robins. Then, solve the puzzle.

Across:

1. One type of food robins eat.

3. The mother robin lays from two to six of these.

4. Robins are _____-looking birds.

6. Another type of food robins eat.

Down:

1. The robin's _____ is sweet and mellow.

2. Robins were first called by this name.

5. Mother and father robins bring this to their babies.

Comprehension: Rodents

You are surrounded by rodents (row-dents)! There are 1,500 different kinds of rodents. One of the most common rodents is the mouse. Rats, gophers (go-furs), and beavers are also rodents. So are squirrels and porcupines (pork-you-pines).

All rodents have long, sharp teeth. These sharp teeth are called *incisors* (in-size-ors). Rodents use these teeth to eat their food. They eat mostly seeds and vegetables. There is one type of rodent some children have as a pet. No, it is not a rat! It is the guinea (ginney) pig.

Directions: Answer these questions about rodents.

1. How many different kinds of rodents are there?

   _____

2. Name seven kinds of rodents.

   1) _____

   2) _____

   3) _____

   4) _____

   5) _____

   6) _____

   7) _____

3. What rodent is sometimes a pet?

   _____

Have you ever smelled a skunk? A skunk's odor helps protect it. The smell comes from scent glands under the skunk's tail. These scent glands make a liquid that smells very bad. The skunk can shoot the liquid 10 feet into the air. The skunk shoots this liquid to protect itself. The skunk arches it back before it shoots.

There are 10 types of skunks. The most common type is black. It has a white stripe down its head and back. It has a black tip on its tail. Some people have skunks for pets. What do you think they have to remove from the skunk before bringing it home?

Directions: Answer these questions about skunks.

1. Tell what you have to do to have a skunk for a pet.

   _____

   _____

2. What would you do if you saw a wild skunk arch its back?

   _____

   Why?

   _____

Making Inferences: Dictionary Mystery

Directions: Below are six dictionary entries with pronunciations and definitions. The only things missing are the entry words. Write the correct entry words. Be sure to spell each word correctly.

Entry word:

_____

(rōz)
A flower that grows on bushes and vines.

Entry word:

_____

(fäks)
A wild animal that lives in the woods.

Entry word:

_____

(lāk)
A body of water that is surrounded by land.

Entry word:

_____

(ra bət)
A small animal that has long ears.

Entry word:

_____

(pē än ō)
A musical instrument that has many keys.

Entry word:

_____

(bās bȯl)
A game played with a bat and a ball.

Directions: Now write the entry words in alphabetical order.

1. _____

2. _____

3. _____

4. _____

5. _____

6. _____

Opposites: An Opposites Poem

Directions: Read the silly poem and then rewrite it below. As you write, change each bold word into its opposite.

In the **beautiful** land of Goop-dee-goo
   Everyone eats a sweet apple stew.
The **boys walk backwards** all day long
   And **whisper** when they sing a song.
   The **girls** are always kind and fair.
They have **big** thumbs and **long** green hair.
   It **never** rains, so **remember** that—
You **won't** need an umbrella or a hat.
   Please **come** along **here** to Goop-dee-goo,
We'll all be looking **out** for you.
          —Peggy Kaye

_____

_____

_____

_____

_____

_____

_____

_____

Homophones

Homophones are words that sound alike but have different meanings or spellings, such as **week** and **weak**.

The Sun and its planets move through the Milky Way. Do you know how fast the sun and planets move? To find out, follow the instructions below.

Directions: Write the correct word in each sentence. Write the number next to each word you choose in the number box, starting on the left. Add up all the numbers.

Come over _____.	hear **10**	here **20**
The wind _____ all night.	blew **25**	blue **15**
I can _____ you.	see **25**	sea **10**
That mouse has a long _____.	tail **15**	tale **10**
We _____ the race!	one **15**	won **30**
Look at my _____ bike.	knew **20**	new **25**
How much does a whale _____?	weigh **20**	way **15**
Put the belt on your _____.	waste **10**	waist **15**

Number Box

____ + ____ + ____ + ____ + ____ + ____ + ____ + ____ = _____

Complete this sentence with the answer from the number box.

The Sun and planets travel _____ miles every second!

Homograph Puzzle

Homographs are words that are spelled the same but have different meanings or pronunciations, such as **bow** (ribbon) and **bow** (of a ship).

Directions: Think of one word that fits both sentences. Write that word in the puzzle.

Across:

2. You _____ go to the show. My birthday is on _____ 11th.

3. I _____ a bluebird. I will _____ the wood.

4. Do not _____ the bus. My teacher is _____ Jones.

5. _____ me the book. Look at the clock's big _____.

8. You have dirt on your _____. A clock has hands and a _____.

9. I will act in a _____. I want to _____ baseball.

Down:

1. Turn on the _____. The bag feels _____.

2. I know what you _____. Be nice! Don't be _____.

6. I will _____the cards. It is a fair _____.

7. They _____ yesterday. It is in my _____ hand.

8. The bird can _____. Don't let that _____ in the house.

Glossary

Comprehension: Understanding what is seen, read, or heard.

Following Directions: Doing what the directions say to do.

Homographs: Words that are spelled the same but have different meanings or pronunciations, such as **bow** (ribbon) and **bow** (of a ship).

Homophones: Two words that sound alike but have different meanings and spellings. Example: **week** and **weak**.

Inference: Using logic to figure out what is unspoken but evident.

Main Idea: The most important idea, or main point, in a sentence, paragraph, or story.

Recalling Details: Being able to pick out and remember the who, what, when, where, why, and how of what is read.

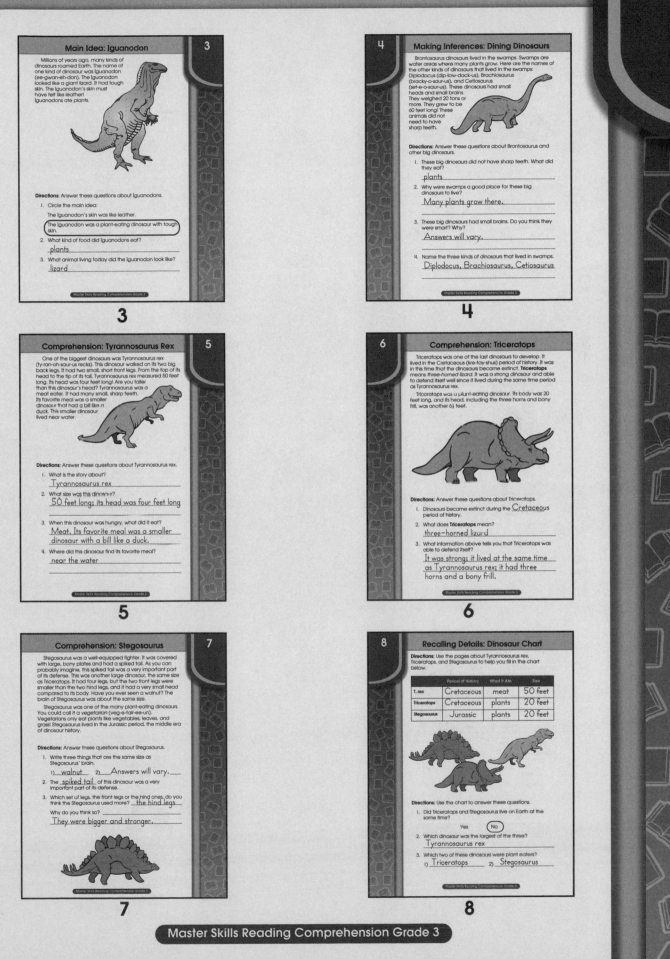

Main Idea: Iguanodon 3

Millions of years ago, many kinds of dinosaurs roamed Earth. The name of one kind of dinosaur was Iguanodon (ee-gwan-eh-don). The Iguanodon looked like a giant lizard. It had tough skin. The Iguanodon's skin must have felt like leather! Iguanodons ate plants.

Directions: Answer these questions about Iguanodons.

1. Circle the main idea:

   The Iguanodon's skin was like leather.

   (The Iguanodon was a plant-eating dinosaur with tough skin.)

2. What kind of food did Iguanodons eat?

   plants

3. What animal living today did the Iguanodon look like?

   lizard

Master Skills Reading Comprehension Grade 3

3

Making Inferences: Dining Dinosaurs 4

Brontosaurus dinosaurs lived in the swamps. Swamps are water areas where many plants grow. Here are the names of the other kinds of dinosaurs that lived in the swamps: Diplodocus (dip-low-dock-us), Brachiosaurus (bracky-o-saur-us), and Cetiosaurus (set-e-o-saur-us). These dinosaurs had small heads and small brains. They weighed 20 tons or more. They grew to be 60 feet long! These animals did not need to have sharp teeth.

Directions: Answer these questions about Brontosaurus and other big dinosaurs.

1. These big dinosaurs did not have sharp teeth. What did they eat?

   plants

2. Why were swamps a good place for these big dinosaurs to live?

   Many plants grow there.

3. These big dinosaurs had small brains. Do you think they were smart? Why?

   Answers will vary.

4. Name the three kinds of dinosaurs that lived in swamps.

   Diplodocus, Brachiosaurus, Cetiosaurus

Master Skills Reading Comprehension Grade 3

4

Comprehension: Tyrannosaurus Rex 5

One of the biggest dinosaurs was Tyrannosaurus rex (ty-ran-oh-saur-us recks). This dinosaur walked on its two big back legs. It had two small, short front legs. From the top of its head to the tip of its tail, Tyrannosaurus rex measured 50 feet long. Its head was four feet long! Are you taller than this dinosaur's head? Tyrannosaurus was a meat eater. It had many small, sharp teeth. Its favorite meal was a smaller dinosaur that had a bill like a duck. This smaller dinosaur lived near water.

Directions: Answer these questions about Tyrannosaurus rex.

1. What is the story about?

   Tyrannosaurus rex

2. What size was this dinosaur?

   50 feet long; its head was four feet long

3. When this dinosaur was hungry, what did it eat?

   Meat. Its favorite meal was a smaller dinosaur with a bill like a duck.

4. Where did this dinosaur find its favorite meal?

   near the water

Master Skills Reading Comprehension Grade 3

5

Comprehension: Triceratops 6

Triceratops was one of the last dinosaurs to develop. It lived in the Cretaceous (kre-tay-shus) period of history. It was in this time that the dinosaurs became extinct. **Triceratops** means *three-horned lizard*. It was a strong dinosaur and able to defend itself well since it lived during the same time period as Tyrannosaurus rex.

Triceratops was a plant-eating dinosaur. Its body was 20 feet long, and its head, including the three horns and bony frill, was another 6½ feet.

Directions: Answer these questions about Triceratops.

1. Dinosaurs became extinct during the Cretaceous period of history.

2. What does **Triceratops** mean?

   three-horned lizard

3. What information above tells you that Triceratops was able to defend itself?

   It was strong; it lived at the same time as Tyrannosaurus rex; it had three horns and a bony frill.

Master Skills Reading Comprehension Grade 3

6

Comprehension: Stegosaurus 7

Stegosaurus was a well-equipped fighter. It was covered with large, bony plates and had a spiked tail. As you can probably imagine, this spiked tail was a very important part of its defense. This was another large dinosaur, the same size as Triceratops. It had four legs, but the two front legs were smaller than the two hind legs, and it had a very small head compared to its body. Have you ever seen a walnut? The brain of Stegosaurus was about the same size.

Stegosaurus was one of the many plant-eating dinosaurs. You could call it a *vegetarian* (veg-e-tair-ee-un). Vegetarians only eat plants like vegetables, leaves, and grass! Stegosaurus lived in the Jurassic period, the middle era of dinosaur history.

Directions: Answer these questions about Stegosaurus.

1. Write three things that are the same size as Stegosaurus' brain.

   1) walnut   2) Answers will vary.

2. The spiked tail of this dinosaur was a very important part of its defense.

3. Which set of legs, the front legs or the hind ones, do you think the Stegosaurus used more? the hind legs

   Why do you think so?

   They were bigger and stronger.

Master Skills Reading Comprehension Grade 3

7

Recalling Details: Dinosaur Chart 8

Directions: Use the pages about Tyrannosaurus rex, Triceratops, and Stegosaurus to help you fill in the chart below.

	Period of History	What It Ate	Size
T. rex	Cretaceous	meat	50 feet
Triceratops	Cretaceous	plants	20 feet
Stegosaurus	Jurassic	plants	20 feet

Directions: Use the chart to answer these questions.

1. Did Triceratops and Stegosaurus live on Earth at the same time?

   Yes   (No)

2. Which dinosaur was the largest of the three?

   Tyrannosaurus rex

3. Which two of these dinosaurs were plant eaters?

   1) Triceratops   2) Stegosaurus

Master Skills Reading Comprehension Grade 3

8

Master Skills Reading Comprehension Grade 3

Answer Key

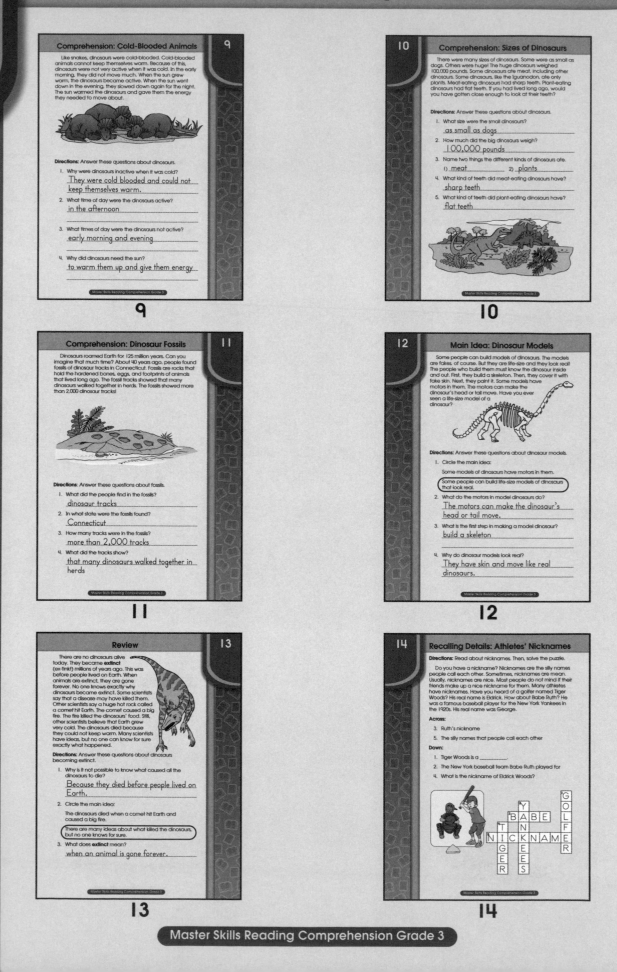

9

Comprehension: Cold-Blooded Animals

Like snakes, dinosaurs were cold-blooded. Cold-blooded animals cannot keep themselves warm. Because of this, dinosaurs were not very active when it was cold. In the early morning, they did not move much. When the sun grew warm, the dinosaurs became active. When the sun went down in the evening, they slowed down again for the night. The sun warmed the dinosaurs and gave them the energy they needed to move about.

Directions: Answer these questions about dinosaurs.

1. Why were dinosaurs inactive when it was cold?
   They were cold blooded and could not keep themselves warm.

2. What time of day were the dinosaurs active?
   in the afternoon

3. What times of day were the dinosaurs not active?
   early morning and evening

4. Why did dinosaurs need the sun?
   to warm them up and give them energy

9

10

Comprehension: Sizes of Dinosaurs

There were many sizes of dinosaurs. Some were as small as dogs. Others were huge! The huge dinosaurs weighed 100,000 pounds. Some dinosaurs ate meat, including other dinosaurs. Some dinosaurs, like the Iguanodon, ate only plants. Meat-eating dinosaurs had sharp teeth. Plant-eating dinosaurs had flat teeth. If you had lived long ago, would you have gotten close enough to look at their teeth?

Directions: Answer these questions about dinosaurs.

1. What size were the small dinosaurs?
   as small as dogs

2. How much did the big dinosaurs weigh?
   100,000 pounds

3. Name two things the different kinds of dinosaurs ate.
   1) meat   2) plants

4. What kind of teeth did meat-eating dinosaurs have?
   sharp teeth

5. What kind of teeth did plant-eating dinosaurs have?
   flat teeth

10

11

Comprehension: Dinosaur Fossils

Dinosaurs roamed Earth for 125 million years. Can you imagine that much time? About 140 years ago, people found fossils of dinosaur tracks in Connecticut. Fossils are rocks that hold the hardened bones, eggs, and footprints of animals that lived long ago. The fossil tracks showed that many dinosaurs walked together in herds. The fossils showed more than 2,000 dinosaur tracks!

Directions: Answer these questions about fossils.

1. What did the people find in the fossils?
   dinosaur tracks

2. In what state were the fossils found?
   Connecticut

3. How many tracks were in the fossils?
   more than 2,000 tracks

4. What did the tracks show?
   that many dinosaurs walked together in herds

11

12

Main Idea: Dinosaur Models

Some people can build models of dinosaurs. The models are fakes, of course. But they are life-size and they look real! The people who build them must know the dinosaur inside and out. First, they build a skeleton. Then, they cover it with fake skin. Next, they paint it. Some models have motors in them. The motors can make the dinosaur's head or tail move. Have you ever seen a life-size model of a dinosaur?

Directions: Answer these questions about dinosaur models.

1. Circle the main idea:

   Some models of dinosaurs have motors in them.

   (Some people can build life-size models of dinosaurs that look real.)

2. What do the motors in model dinosaurs do?
   The motors can make the dinosaur's head or tail move.

3. What is the first step in making a model dinosaur?
   build a skeleton

4. Why do dinosaur models look real?
   They have skin and move like real dinosaurs.

12

13

Review

There are no dinosaurs alive today. They became **extinct** (ex-tinkt) millions of years ago. This was before people lived on Earth. When animals are extinct, they are gone forever. No one knows exactly why dinosaurs became extinct. Some scientists say that a disease may have killed them. Other scientists say a huge hot rock called a comet hit Earth. The comet caused a big fire. The fire killed the dinosaurs' food. Still, other scientists believe that Earth grew very cold. The dinosaurs died because they could not keep warm. Many scientists have ideas, but no one can know for sure exactly what happened.

Directions: Answer these questions about dinosaurs becoming extinct.

1. Why is it not possible to know what caused all the dinosaurs to die?
   Because they died before people lived on Earth.

2. Circle the main idea:

   The dinosaurs died when a comet hit Earth and caused a big fire.

   (There are many ideas about what killed the dinosaurs, but no one knows for sure.)

3. What does **extinct** mean?
   when an animal is gone forever.

13

14

Recalling Details: Athletes' Nicknames

Directions: Read about nicknames. Then, solve the puzzle.

Do you have a nickname? Nicknames are the silly names people call each other. Sometimes, nicknames are mean. Usually, nicknames are nice. Most people do not mind if their friends make up a nice nickname for them. Many athletes have nicknames. Have you heard of a golfer named Tiger Woods? His real name is Eldrick. How about Babe Ruth? He was a famous baseball player for the New York Yankees in the 1920s. His real name was George.

Across:

3. Ruth's nickname

5. The silly names that people call each other

Down:

1. Tiger Woods is a _____.

2. The New York baseball team Babe Ruth played for

4. What is the nickname of Eldrick Woods?

Crossword answers: BABE, GOLFER, YANKEES, NICKNAME, TIGER

14

Answer Key

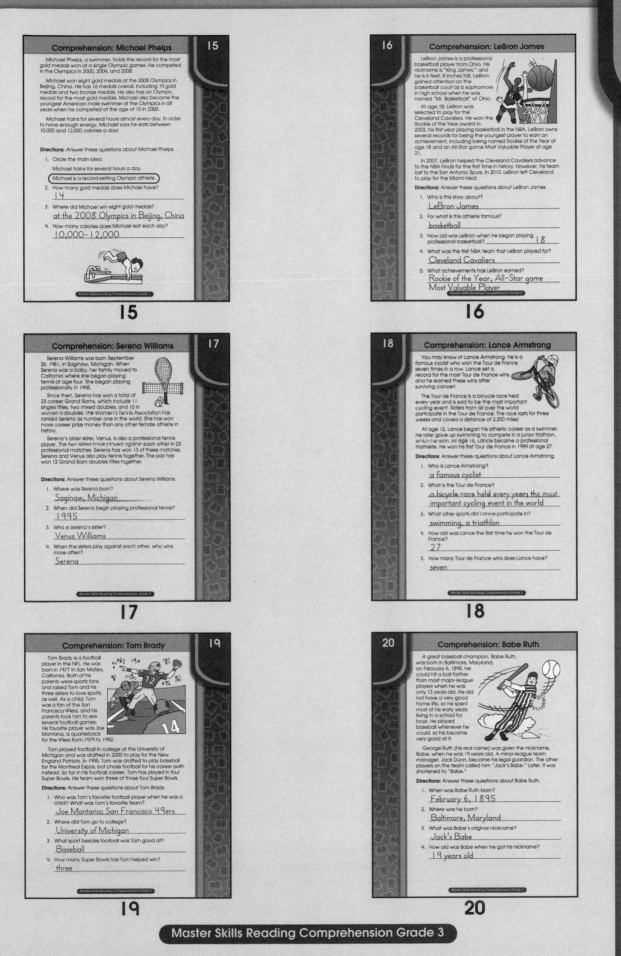

Comprehension: Michael Phelps — 15

Michael Phelps, a swimmer, holds the record for the most gold medals won at a single Olympic games. He competed in the Olympics in 2000, 2004, and 2008.

Michael won eight gold medals at the 2008 Olympics in Beijing, China. He has 16 medals overall, including 14 gold medals and two bronze medals. He also has an Olympic record for the most gold medals. Michael also became the youngest American male swimmer at the Olympics in 68 years when he competed at the age of 15 in 2000.

Michael trains for several hours almost every day. In order to have enough energy, Michael says he eats between 10,000 and 12,000 calories a day!

Directions: Answer these questions about Michael Phelps.

1. Circle the main idea:

   Michael trains for several hours a day.

   (Michael is a record-setting Olympic athlete.)

2. How many gold medals does Michael have?

   14

3. Where did Michael win eight gold medals?

   at the 2008 Olympics in Beijing, China

4. How many calories does Michael eat each day?

   10,000-12,000

15

Comprehension: LeBron James — 16

LeBron James is a professional basketball player from Ohio. His nickname is "King James," and he is 6 feet, 8 inches tall. LeBron gained attention on the basketball court as a sophomore in high school when he was named "Mr. Basketball" of Ohio.

At age 18, LeBron was selected to play for the Cleveland Cavaliers. He won the Rookie of the Year award in 2003, his first year playing basketball in the NBA. LeBron owns several records for being the youngest player to earn an achievement, including being named Rookie of the Year at age 18 and an All-Star game Most Valuable Player at age 21.

In 2007, LeBron helped the Cleveland Cavaliers advance to the NBA Finals for the first time in history. However, his team lost to the San Antonio Spurs. In 2010, LeBron left Cleveland to play for the Miami Heat.

Directions: Answer these questions about LeBron James.

1. Who is this story about?

   LeBron James

2. For what is this athlete famous?

   basketball

3. How old was LeBron when he began playing professional basketball? 18

4. What was the first NBA team that LeBron played for?

   Cleveland Cavaliers

5. What achievements has LeBron earned?

   Rookie of the Year, All-Star game Most Valuable Player

16

Comprehension: Serena Williams — 17

Serena Williams was born September 26, 1981, in Saginaw, Michigan. When Serena was a baby, her family moved to California where she began playing tennis at age four. She began playing professionally in 1995.

Since then, Serena has won a total of 23 career Grand Slams, which include 11 singles titles, two mixed doubles, and 10 in women's doubles. The Women's Tennis Association has ranked Serena as number one in the world. She has won more career prize money than any other female athlete in history.

Serena's older sister, Venus, is also a professional tennis player. The two sisters have played against each other in 23 professional matches. Serena has won 13 of these matches. Serena and Venus also play tennis together. The pair has won 12 Grand Slam doubles titles together.

Directions: Answer these questions about Serena Williams.

1. Where was Serena born?

   Saginaw, Michigan

2. When did Serena begin playing professional tennis?

   1995

3. Who is Serena's sister?

   Venus Williams

4. When the sisters play against each other, who wins more often?

   Serena

17

Comprehension: Lance Armstrong — 18

You may know of Lance Armstrong. He is a famous cyclist who won the Tour de France seven times in a row. Lance set a record for the most Tour de France wins, and he earned these wins after surviving cancer!

The Tour de France is a bicycle race held every year and is said to be the most important cycling event. Riders from all over the world participate in the Tour de France. The race lasts for three weeks and covers a distance of 2,200 miles!

At age 12, Lance began his athletic career as a swimmer. He later gave up swimming to compete in a junior triathlon, which he won. At age 16, Lance became a professional triathlete. He won his first Tour de France in 1999 at age 27.

Directions: Answer these questions about Lance Armstrong.

1. Who is Lance Armstrong?

   a famous cyclist

2. What is the Tour de France?

   a bicycle race held every year; the most important cycling event in the world

3. What other sports did Lance participate in?

   swimming, a triathlon

4. How old was Lance the first time he won the Tour de France?

   27

5. How many Tour de France wins does Lance have?

   seven

18

Comprehension: Tom Brady — 19

Tom Brady is a football player in the NFL. He was born in 1977 in San Mateo, California. Both of his parents were sports fans and raised Tom and his three sisters to love sports, as well. As a child, Tom was a fan of the San Francisco 49ers, and his parents took him to see several football games. His favorite player was Joe Montana, a quarterback for the 49ers from 1979 to 1992.

Tom played football in college at the University of Michigan and was drafted in 2000 to play for the New England Patriots. In 1995, Tom was drafted to play baseball for the Montreal Expos, but chose football for his career path instead. So far in his football career, Tom has played in four Super Bowls. His team won three of those four Super Bowls.

Directions: Answer these questions about Tom Brady.

1. Who was Tom's favorite football player when he was a child? What was Tom's favorite team?

   Joe Montana; San Francisco 49ers

2. Where did Tom go to college?

   University of Michigan

3. What sport besides football was Tom good at?

   Baseball

4. How many Super Bowls has Tom helped win?

   three

19

Comprehension: Babe Ruth — 20

A great baseball champion, Babe Ruth, was born in Baltimore, Maryland, on February 6, 1895. He could hit a ball farther than most major-league players when he was only 13 years old. He did not have a very good home life, so he spent most of his early years living in a school for boys. He played baseball whenever he could, so he became very good at it.

George Ruth (his real name) was given the nickname, Babe, when he was 19 years old. A minor-league team manager, Jack Dunn, became his legal guardian. The other players on the team called him "Jack's Babe." Later, it was shortened to "Babe."

Directions: Answer these questions about Babe Ruth.

1. When was Babe Ruth born?

   February 6, 1895

2. Where was he born?

   Baltimore, Maryland

3. What was Babe's original nickname?

   Jack's Babe

4. How old was Babe when he got his nickname?

   19 years old

20

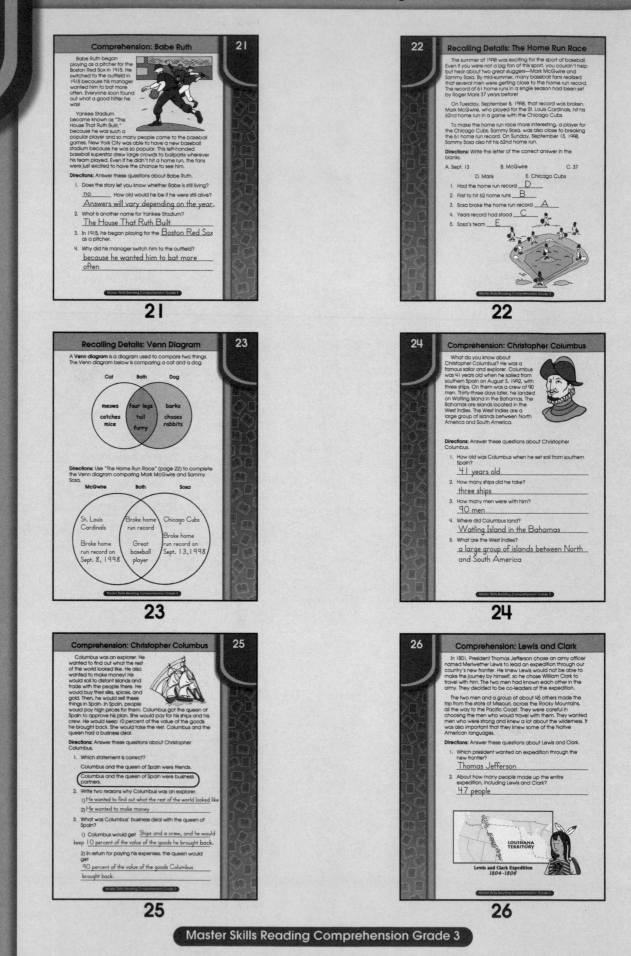

21

Comprehension: Babe Ruth

Babe Ruth began playing as a pitcher for the Boston Red Sox in 1915. He switched to the outfield in 1918 because his manager wanted him to bat more often. Everyone soon found out what a good hitter he was!

Yankee Stadium became known as "The House That Ruth Built," because he was such a popular player and so many people came to the baseball games. New York City was able to have a new baseball stadium because he was so popular. This left-handed baseball superstar drew large crowds to ballparks wherever his team played. Even if he didn't hit a home run, the fans were just excited to have the chance to see him.

Directions: Answer these questions about Babe Ruth.

1. Does the story let you know whether Babe is still living?
   __no__ How old would he be if he were still alive?
   __Answers will vary depending on the year.__

2. What is another name for Yankee Stadium?
   __The House That Ruth Built__

3. In 1915, he began playing for the __Boston Red Sox__ as a pitcher.

4. Why did his manager switch him to the outfield?
   __because he wanted him to bat more__
   __often__

21

22

Recalling Details: The Home Run Race

The summer of 1998 was exciting for the sport of baseball. Even if you were not a big fan of this sport, you couldn't help but hear about two great sluggers—Mark McGwire and Sammy Sosa. By mid-summer, many baseball fans realized that several men were getting close to the home run record. The record of 61 home runs in a single season had been set by Roger Maris 37 years before!

On Tuesday, September 8, 1998, that record was broken. Mark McGwire, who played for the St. Louis Cardinals, hit his 62nd home run in a game with the Chicago Cubs.

To make the home run race more interesting, a player for the Chicago Cubs, Sammy Sosa, was also close to breaking the 61 home run record. On Sunday, September 13, 1998, Sammy Sosa also hit his 62nd home run.

Directions: Write the letter of the correct answer in the blanks.

A. Sept. 13   B. McGwire   C. 37
   D. Maris   E. Chicago Cubs

1. Had the home run record   __D__
2. First to hit 62 home runs   __B__
3. Sosa broke the home run record   __A__
4. Years record had stood   __C__
5. Sosa's team   __E__

22

23

Recalling Details: Venn Diagram

A **Venn diagram** is a diagram used to compare two things. The Venn diagram below is comparing a cat and a dog.

Cat — meows, catches mice
Both — four legs, tail, furry
Dog — barks, chases rabbits

Directions: Use "The Home Run Race" (page 22) to complete the Venn diagram comparing Mark McGwire and Sammy Sosa.

McGwire — St. Louis Cardinals, Broke home run record on Sept. 8, 1998
Both — Broke home run record, Great baseball player
Sosa — Chicago Cubs, Broke home run record on Sept. 13, 1998

23

24

Comprehension: Christopher Columbus

What do you know about Christopher Columbus? He was a famous sailor and explorer. Columbus was 41 years old when he sailed from southern Spain on August 3, 1492, with three ships. On them was a crew of 90 men. Thirty-three days later, he landed on Watling Island in the Bahamas. The Bahamas are islands located in the West Indies. The West Indies are a large group of islands between North America and South America.

Directions: Answer these questions about Christopher Columbus.

1. How old was Columbus when he set sail from southern Spain?
   __41 years old__

2. How many ships did he take?
   __three ships__

3. How many men were with him?
   __90 men__

4. Where did Columbus land?
   __Watling Island in the Bahamas__

5. What are the West Indies?
   __a large group of islands between North__
   __and South America__

24

25

Comprehension: Christopher Columbus

Columbus was an explorer. He wanted to find out what the rest of the world looked like. He also wanted to make money! He would sail to distant islands and trade with the people there. He would buy their silks, spices, and gold. Then, he would sell these things in Spain. In Spain, people would pay high prices for them. Columbus got the queen of Spain to approve his plan. She would pay for his ships and his crew. He would keep 10 percent of the value of the goods he brought back. She would take the rest. Columbus and the queen had a business deal.

Directions: Answer these questions about Christopher Columbus.

1. Which statement is correct?
   Columbus and the queen of Spain were friends.
   (Columbus and the queen of Spain were business partners.)

2. Write two reasons why Columbus was an explorer.
   1) He wanted to find out what the rest of the world looked like
   2) He wanted to make money

3. What was Columbus' business deal with the queen of Spain?
   1) Columbus would get __Ships and a crew, and he would__ keep __10__ percent of the value of the goods he brought back.

   2) In return for paying his expenses, the queen would get
   __90__ percent of the value of the goods Columbus brought back.

25

26

Comprehension: Lewis and Clark

In 1801, President Thomas Jefferson chose an army officer named Meriwether Lewis to lead an expedition through our country's new frontier. He knew Lewis would not be able to make the journey by himself, so he chose William Clark to travel with him. The two men had known each other in the army. They decided to be co-leaders of the expedition.

The two men and a group of about 45 others made the trip from the state of Missouri, across the Rocky Mountains, all the way to the Pacific Coast. They were careful in choosing the men who would travel with them. They wanted men who were strong and knew a lot about the wilderness. It was also important that they knew some of the Native American languages.

Directions: Answer these questions about Lewis and Clark.

1. Which president wanted an expedition through the new frontier?
   __Thomas Jefferson__

2. About how many people made up the entire expedition, including Lewis and Clark?
   __47 people__

LOUISIANA TERRITORY

Lewis and Clark Expedition
1804-1806

26

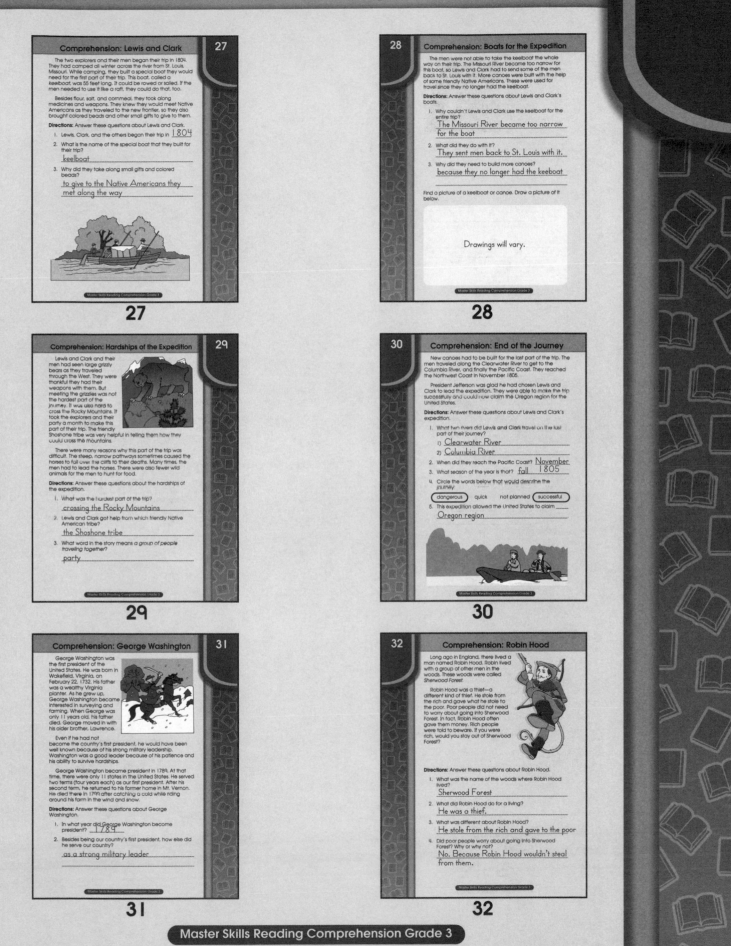

Comprehension: Lewis and Clark — 27

The two explorers and their men began their trip in 1804. They had camped all winter across the river from St. Louis, Missouri. While camping, they built a special boat they would need for the first part of their trip. This boat, called a *keelboat*, was 55 feet long. It could be rowed or sailed. If the men needed to use it like a raft, they could do that, too.

Besides flour, salt, and cornmeal, they took along medicines and weapons. They knew they would meet Native Americans as they traveled to the new frontier, so they also brought colored beads and other small gifts to give to them.

Directions: Answer these questions about Lewis and Clark.

1. Lewis, Clark, and the others began their trip in <u>1804</u>

2. What is the name of the special boat that they built for their trip?
<u>keelboat</u>

3. Why did they take along small gifts and colored beads?
<u>to give to the Native Americans they met along the way</u>

27

Comprehension: Boats for the Expedition — 28

The men were not able to take the keelboat the whole way on their trip. The Missouri River became too narrow for this boat, so Lewis and Clark had to send some of the men back to St. Louis with it. More canoes were built with the help of some friendly Native Americans. These were used for travel since they no longer had the keelboat.

Directions: Answer these questions about Lewis and Clark's boats.

1. Why couldn't Lewis and Clark use the keelboat for the entire trip?
<u>The Missouri River became too narrow for the boat</u>

2. What did they do with it?
<u>They sent men back to St. Louis with it.</u>

3. Why did they need to build more canoes?
<u>because they no longer had the keelboat</u>

Find a picture of a keelboat or canoe. Draw a picture of it below.

Drawings will vary.

28

Comprehension: Hardships of the Expedition — 29

Lewis and Clark and their men had seen large grizzly bears as they traveled through the West. They were thankful they had their weapons with them. But meeting the grizzlies was not the hardest part of the journey. It was also hard to cross the Rocky Mountains. It took the explorers and their party a month to make this part of their trip. The friendly Shoshone tribe was very helpful in telling them how they could cross the mountains.

There were many reasons why this part of the trip was difficult. The steep, narrow pathways sometimes caused the horses to fall over the cliffs to their deaths. Many times, the men had to lead the horses. There were also fewer wild animals for the men to hunt for food.

Directions: Answer these questions about the hardships of the expedition.

1. What was the hardest part of the trip?
<u>crossing the Rocky Mountains</u>

2. Lewis and Clark got help from which friendly Native American tribe?
<u>the Shoshone tribe</u>

3. What word in the story means *a group of people traveling together*?
<u>party</u>

29

Comprehension: End of the Journey — 30

New canoes had to be built for the last part of the trip. The men traveled along the Clearwater River to get to the Columbia River, and finally the Pacific Coast. They reached the Northwest Coast in November 1805.

President Jefferson was glad he had chosen Lewis and Clark to lead the expedition. They were able to make the trip successfully and could now claim the Oregon region for the United States.

Directions: Answer these questions about Lewis and Clark's expedition.

1. What two rivers did Lewis and Clark travel on the last part of their journey?
   1) <u>Clearwater River</u>
   2) <u>Columbia River</u>

2. When did they reach the Pacific Coast? <u>November 1805</u>

3. What season of the year is that? <u>fall</u>

4. Circle the words below that would describe the journey!
   (dangerous)   quick   not planned   (successful)

5. This expedition allowed the United States to claim <u>Oregon region</u>

30

Comprehension: George Washington — 31

George Washington was the first president of the United States. He was born in Wakefield, Virginia, on February 22, 1732. His father was a wealthy Virginia planter. As he grew up, George Washington became interested in surveying and farming. When George was only 11 years old, his father died. George moved in with his older brother, Lawrence.

Even if he had not become the country's first president, he would have been well known because of his strong military leadership. Washington was a good leader because of his patience and his ability to survive hardships.

George Washington became president in 1789. At that time, there were only 11 states in the United States. He served two terms (four years each) as our first president. After his second term, he returned to his former home in Mt. Vernon. He died there in 1799 after catching a cold while riding around his farm in the wind and snow.

Directions: Answer these questions about George Washington.

1. In what year did George Washington become president? <u>1789</u>

2. Besides being our country's first president, how else did he serve our country?
<u>as a strong military leader</u>

31

Comprehension: Robin Hood — 32

Long ago in England, there lived a man named Robin Hood. Robin lived with a group of other men in the woods. These woods were called *Sherwood Forest*.

Robin Hood was a thief—a different kind of thief. He stole from the rich and gave what he stole to the poor. Poor people did not need to worry about going into Sherwood Forest. In fact, Robin Hood often gave them money. Rich people were told to beware. If you were rich, would you stay out of Sherwood Forest?

Directions: Answer these questions about Robin Hood.

1. What was the name of the woods where Robin Hood lived?
<u>Sherwood Forest</u>

2. What did Robin Hood do for a living?
<u>He was a thief.</u>

3. What was different about Robin Hood?
<u>He stole from the rich and gave to the poor</u>

4. Did poor people worry about going into Sherwood Forest? Why or why not?
<u>No. Because Robin Hood wouldn't steal from them.</u>

32

Answer Key

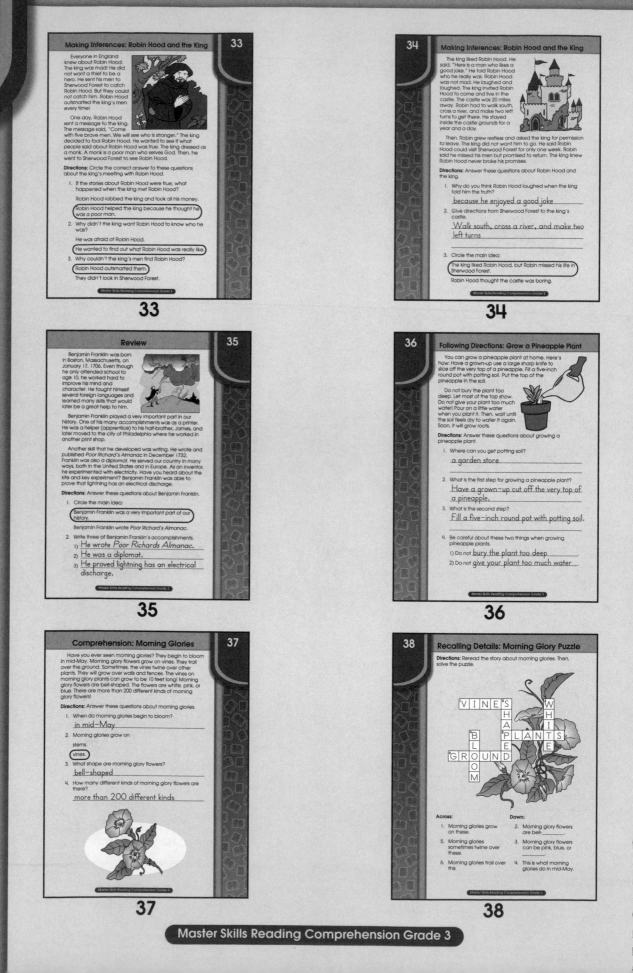

Making Inferences: Robin Hood and the King · 33

Everyone in England knew about Robin Hood. The king was mad! He did not want him to be a hero. He sent his men to Sherwood Forest to catch Robin Hood. But they could not catch him. Robin Hood outsmarted the king's men every time!

One day, Robin Hood sent a message to the king. The message said, "Come with five brave men. We will see who is stronger." The king decided to fool Robin Hood. He wanted to see if what people said about Robin Hood was true. The king dressed as a monk. A monk is a poor man who serves God. Then, he went to Sherwood Forest to see Robin Hood.

Directions: Circle the correct answer to these questions about the king's meeting with Robin Hood.

1. If the stories about Robin Hood were true, what happened when the king met Robin Hood?

   Robin Hood robbed the king and took all his money.

   (Robin Hood helped the king because he thought he was a poor man.)

2. Why didn't the king want Robin Hood to know who he was?

   He was afraid of Robin Hood.

   (He wanted to find out what Robin Hood was really like.)

3. Why couldn't the king's men find Robin Hood?

   (Robin Hood outsmarted them.)

   They didn't look in Sherwood Forest.

33

---

34 · **Making Inferences: Robin Hood and the King**

The king liked Robin Hood. He said, "Here is a man who likes a good joke." He told Robin Hood who he really was. Robin Hood was not mad. He laughed and laughed. The king invited Robin Hood to come and live in the castle. The castle was 20 miles away. Robin had to walk south, cross a river, and make two left turns to get there. He stayed inside the castle grounds for a year and a day.

Then, Robin grew restless and asked the king for permission to leave. The king did not want him to go. He said Robin Hood could visit Sherwood Forest for only one week. Robin said he missed his men but promised to return. The king knew Robin Hood never broke his promises.

Directions: Answer these questions about Robin Hood and the king.

1. Why do you think Robin Hood laughed when the king told him the truth?

   because he enjoyed a good joke

2. Give directions from Sherwood Forest to the king's castle.

   Walk south, cross a river, and make two left turns

3. Circle the main idea:

   (The king liked Robin Hood, but Robin missed his life in Sherwood Forest.)

   Robin Hood thought the castle was boring.

34

Review · 35

Benjamin Franklin was born in Boston, Massachusetts, on January 17, 1706. Even though he only attended school to age 10, he worked hard to improve his mind and character. He taught himself several foreign languages and learned many skills that would later be a great help to him.

Benjamin Franklin played a very important part in our history. One of his many accomplishments was as a printer. He was a helper (apprentice) to his half-brother, James, and later moved to the city of Philadelphia where he worked in another print shop.

Another skill that he developed was writing. He wrote and published *Poor Richard's Almanac* in December 1732. Franklin was also a diplomat. He served our country in many ways, both in the United States and in Europe. As an inventor, he experimented with electricity. Have you heard about the kite and key experiment? Benjamin Franklin was able to prove that lightning has an electrical discharge.

Directions: Answer these questions about Benjamin Franklin.

1. Circle the main idea:

   (Benjamin Franklin was a very important part of our history.)

   Benjamin Franklin wrote *Poor Richard's Almanac*.

2. Write three of Benjamin Franklin's accomplishments.

   1) He wrote *Poor Richards Almanac*.
   2) He was a diplomat.
   3) He proved lightning has an electrical discharge.

35

---

36 · **Following Directions: Grow a Pineapple Plant**

You can grow a pineapple plant at home. Here's how: Have a grown-up use a large sharp knife to slice off the very top of a pineapple. Fill a five-inch round pot with potting soil. Put the top of the pineapple in the soil.

Do not bury the plant too deep. Let most of the top show. Do not give your plant too much water! Pour on a little water when you plant it. Then, wait until the soil feels dry to water it again. Soon, it will grow roots.

Directions: Answer these questions about growing a pineapple plant.

1. Where can you get potting soil?

   a garden store

2. What is the first step for growing a pineapple plant?

   Have a grown-up cut off the very top of a pineapple.

3. What is the second step?

   Fill a five-inch round pot with potting soil.

4. Be careful about these two things when growing pineapple plants.

   1) Do not bury the plant too deep
   2) Do not give your plant too much water

36

Comprehension: Morning Glories · 37

Have you ever seen morning glories? They begin to bloom in mid-May. Morning glory flowers grow on vines. They trail over the ground. Sometimes, the vines twine over other plants. They will grow over walls and fences. The vines on morning glory plants can grow to be 10 feet long! Morning glory flowers are bell-shaped. The flowers are white, pink, or blue. There are more than 200 different kinds of morning glory flowers!

Directions: Answer these questions about morning glories.

1. When do morning glories begin to bloom?

   in mid-May

2. Morning glories grow on stems.

   (vines.)

3. What shape are morning glory flowers?

   bell-shaped

4. How many different kinds of morning glory flowers are there?

   more than 200 different kinds

37

---

38 · **Recalling Details: Morning Glory Puzzle**

Directions: Reread the story about morning glories. Then, solve the puzzle.

```
V I N E S      W H I
          H    P     I
      B   A    L     T
      L   P    A     E
      O   GROUND N
      O          T
      M          S
```

V I N E S / S H A P E / W H I T E / B L O O M / P L A N T S / G R O U N D / B L U E

Across:

1. Morning glories grow on these.
5. Morning glories sometimes twine over these.
6. Morning glories trail over this

Down:

2. Morning glory flowers are bell-_____.
3. Morning glory flowers can be pink, blue, or _____.
4. This is what morning glories do in mid-May.

38

Answer Key

115

---

39 — Following Directions: How Plants Get Food

Every living thing needs food. Did you ever wonder how plants get food? They do not sit down and eat a bowl of soup! Plants get their food from the soil and from water. To see how, cut off some stalks of celery. Put the stalks in a clear glass. Fill the glass half full of water. Add a few drops of red food coloring to the water. Leave it overnight. The next day, you will see that parts of the celery have turned red! The red lines show how the celery sucked up the water.

Directions: Answer these questions about how plants get food.

1. Name two ways plants get food.
   1) _from soil_
   2) _from water_
2. Complete the four steps for using celery to see how plants get food.
   1) Cut off some stalks of _celery_
   2) Put the stalks in _a clear glass_
   3) Fill the glass _half full of water_
   4) Add a few drops of _red food coloring to the water_
3. What do the red lines in the celery show?
   how the celery sucked up the water

39

---

40 — Making Inferences: Fig Marigolds

Fig marigolds are beautiful! The flowers stay closed unless the light is bright. These flowers are also called by another name—the *mid-day flower*. Mid-day flowers have very long leaves. The leaves are as long as your finger!

There is something else unusual about mid-day flowers. They change color. When the flowers bloom, they are light yellow. After two or three days, they turn pink.

Mid-day flowers grow in California and South America where it is hot. They do not grow in other parts of the United States.

Directions: Answer these questions about fig marigolds.

1. Why do you think fig marigolds are also called mid-day flowers?
   because the flowers stay closed unless the light is bright
2. How long are the leaves of the mid-day flower?
   as long as your finger
3. Why do you think mid-day flowers do not grow all over the United States?
   because they need hot weather to grow

40

---

41 — Comprehension: Rainforests

The soil in rainforests is very dark and rich. The trees and plants that grow there are very green. People who have seen one say a rainforest is "the greenest place on Earth." Why? Because it rains a lot. With so much rain, the plants stay very green. The ground stays very wet. Rainforests cover only 6 percent of Earth. But they are home to 66 percent of all the different kinds of plants and animals on Earth! Today, rainforests are threatened by such things as acid rain from factory smoke emissions around the world, and from farm expansion. Farmers living near rainforests cut down many trees each year to clear the land for farming. I wish I could see a rainforest. Do you?

Directions: Answer these questions about rainforests.

1. What do the plants and trees in a rainforest look like?
   They are very green.
2. What is the soil like in a rainforest?
   very dark and rich
3. How much of the Earth is covered by rainforests?
   6 percent
4. What percentage of Earth's plants and animals live there?
   66 percent

41

---

42 — Comprehension: The Rainforest Lizard

Many strange animals live in the rainforest. One kind of strange animal is a very large lizard. This lizard grows as large as a dog! It has scales on its skin. It has a very wide mouth. It has spikes sticking out of the top of its head. It looks scary, but don't be afraid! This lizard eats mostly weeds. This lizard does not look very tasty, but other animals think it tastes good. Snakes eat these lizards. So do certain birds. Some people in the rainforest eat them, too! Would you like to eat a lizard for lunch?

Directions: Answer these questions about the rainforest lizard.

1. What is the size of this rainforest lizard?
   as large as a dog
2. Where do its scales grow?
   on its skin
3. Which kind of food does the lizard eat?
   mostly weeds
4. Who likes to eat these lizards?
   snakes, birds, and some people

42

---

43 — Comprehension: The Sloth

The sloth spends most of its life in the trees of the rainforest. The three-toed sloth, for example, is usually hanging around, using its claws to keep it there. Because it is in the trees so much, it has trouble moving on the ground. Certainly it could be caught easily by other animals of the rainforest if it was being chased. The sloth is a very slow-moving animal.

Do you have any idea what the sloth eats? The sloth eats mostly leaves it finds in the treetops.

Have you ever seen a three- or two-toed sloth? If you see one in a zoo, you don't have to get close enough to count the toes. You can tell these two cousins apart in a different way—the three-toed sloth has some green mixed in with its fur because of the algae it gets from the trees.

Directions: Answer these questions about the sloth.

1. How does the three-toed sloth hang around the rainforest?
   a. by its tail, like a monkey
   (b. by its claws, or toes)
2. The main diet of the sloth is _leaves_
3. Why does the sloth have trouble moving around on the ground?
   because it is in the trees so much

43

---

44 — Comprehension: The Kinkajou

If you have ever seen a raccoon holding its food by its hands and carefully eating it, you would have an idea of how the kinkajou (king-kuh-joo) eats. This animal of the rainforest is a cousin of the raccoon. Unlike its North American cousin, though, it is a golden-brown color.

The kinkajou's head and body are 17 to 22 inches long. The long tail of the kinkajou comes in handy for hanging around its neighborhood! If you do some quick mental math you can get a good idea of its size. It weighs very little—about five pounds. (You may have a five-pound bag of sugar or flour in your kitchen to help you get an idea of the kinkajou's weight.)

This rainforest animal eats a variety of things. It enjoys nectar from the many rainforest flowers, insects, fruit, honey, birds, and other small animals. Because it lives mostly in the trees, the kinkajou has a ready supply of food.

Directions: Answer these questions about the kinkajou.

1. The kinkajou is a cousin to the _raccoon_
2. Write three things the kinkajou eats.
   1) _nectar_   Answers will vary but may include
   2) _insects_
   3) _fruit_

44

Master Skills Reading Comprehension Grade 3

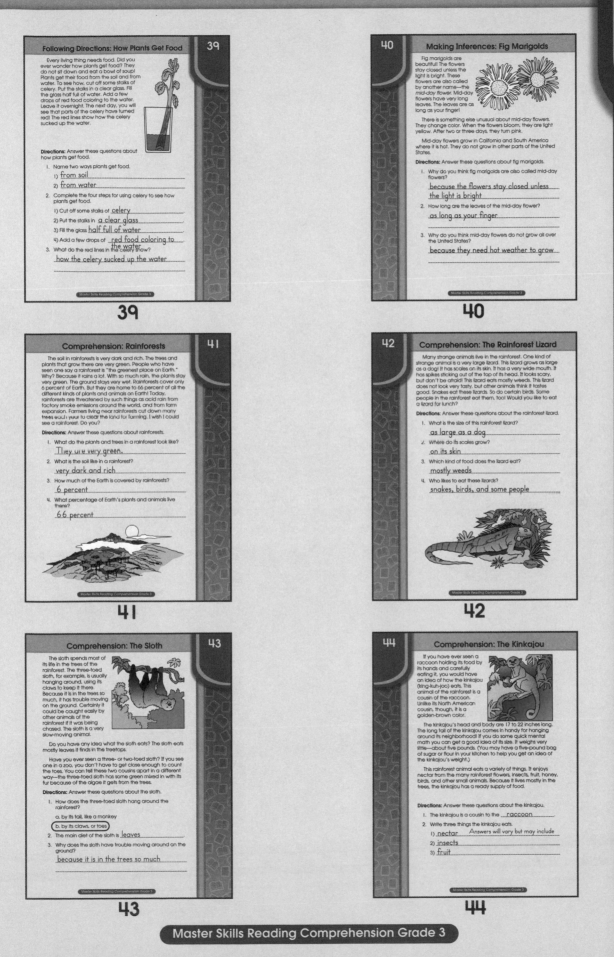

Answer Key

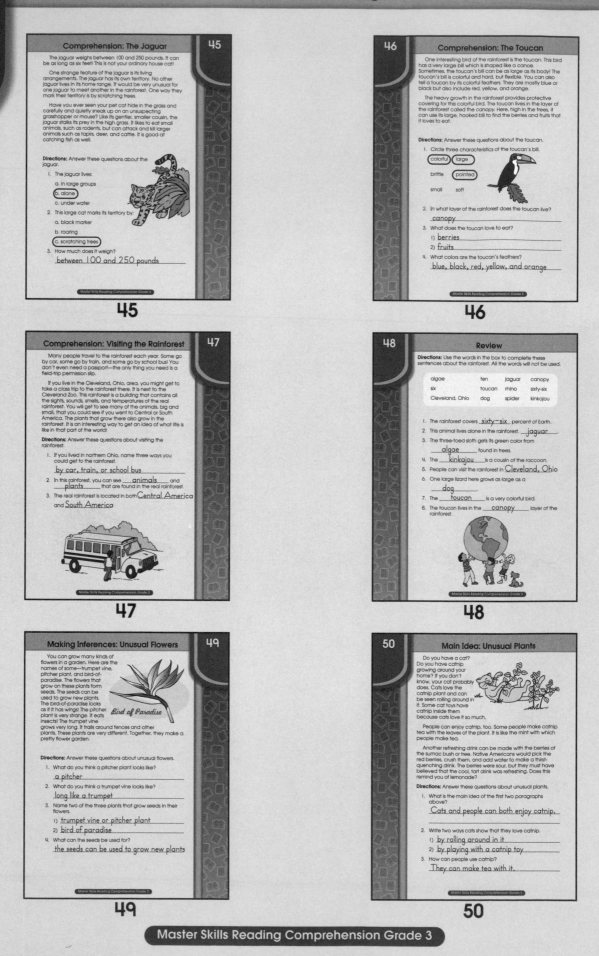

45

Comprehension: The Jaguar

The jaguar weighs between 100 and 250 pounds. It can be as long as six feet! This is not your ordinary house cat!

One strange feature of the jaguar is its living arrangements. The jaguar has its own territory. No other jaguar lives in its home range. It would be very unusual for one jaguar to meet another in the rainforest. One way they mark their territory is by scratching trees.

Have you ever seen your pet cat hide in the grass and carefully and quietly sneak up on an unsuspecting grasshopper or mouse? Like its gentler, smaller cousin, the jaguar stalks its prey in the high grass. It likes to eat small animals, such as rodents, but can attack and kill larger animals such as tapirs, deer, and cattle. It is good at catching fish as well.

Directions: Answer these questions about the jaguar.

1. The jaguar lives:
   a. in large groups
   b. alone ⟵
   c. under water

2. This large cat marks its territory by:
   a. black marker
   b. roaring
   c. scratching trees ⟵

3. How much does it weigh?
   between 100 and 250 pounds

45

46

Comprehension: The Toucan

One interesting bird of the rainforest is the toucan. This bird has a very large bill which is shaped like a canoe. Sometimes, the toucan's bill can be as large as its body! The toucan's bill is colorful and hard, but flexible. You can also tell a toucan by its colorful feathers. They are mostly blue or black but also include red, yellow, and orange.

The heavy growth in the rainforest provides protective covering for this colorful bird. The toucan lives in the layer of the rainforest called the canopy. Here, high in the trees, it can use its large, hooked bill to find the berries and fruits that it loves to eat.

Directions: Answer these questions about the toucan.

1. Circle three characteristics of the toucan's bill.
   (colorful) (large)
   brittle (pointed)
   small soft

2. In what layer of the rainforest does the toucan live?
   canopy

3. What does the toucan love to eat?
   1) berries
   2) fruits

4. What colors are the toucan's feathers?
   blue, black, red, yellow, and orange

46

47

Comprehension: Visiting the Rainforest

Many people travel to the rainforest each year. Some go by car, some go by train, and some go by school bus! You don't even need a passport—the only thing you need is a field-trip permission slip.

If you live in the Cleveland, Ohio, area, you might get to take a class trip to the rainforest there. It is next to the Cleveland Zoo. This rainforest is a building that contains all the sights, sounds, smells, and temperatures of the real rainforest. You will get to see many of the animals, big and small, that you could see if you went to Central or South America. The plants that grow there also grow in the rainforest. It is an interesting way to get an idea of what life is like in that part of the world!

Directions: Answer these questions about visiting the rainforest.

1. If you lived in northern Ohio, name three ways you could get to the rainforest.
   by car, train, or school bus

2. In this rainforest, you can see animals and plants that are found in the real rainforest.

3. The real rainforest is located in both Central America and South America

47

48

Review

Directions: Use the words in the box to complete these sentences about the rainforest. All the words will not be used.

algae	ten	jaguar	canopy
six	toucan	rhino	sixty-six
Cleveland, Ohio	dog	spider	kinkajou

1. The rainforest covers sixty-six percent of Earth.
2. This animal lives alone in the rainforest. jaguar
3. The three-toed sloth gets its green color from algae found in trees.
4. The kinkajou is a cousin of the raccoon.
5. People can visit the rainforest in Cleveland, Ohio
6. One large lizard here grows as large as a dog
7. The toucan is a very colorful bird.
8. The toucan lives in the canopy layer of the rainforest.

48

49

Making Inferences: Unusual Flowers

You can grow many kinds of flowers in a garden. Here are the names of some—trumpet vine, pitcher plant, and bird-of-paradise. The flowers that grow on these plants form seeds. The seeds can be used to grow new plants. The bird-of-paradise looks as if it has wings! The pitcher plant is very strange. It eats insects! The trumpet vine grows very long. It trails around fences and other plants. These plants are very different. Together, they make a pretty flower garden.

Bird of Paradise

Directions: Answer these questions about unusual flowers.

1. What do you think a pitcher plant looks like?
   a pitcher

2. What do you think a trumpet vine looks like?
   long like a trumpet

3. Name two of the three plants that grow seeds in their flowers.
   1) trumpet vine or pitcher plant
   2) bird of paradise

4. What can the seeds be used for?
   the seeds can be used to grow new plants

49

50

Main Idea: Unusual Plants

Do you have a cat? Do you have catnip growing around your home? If you don't know, your cat probably does. Cats love the catnip plant and can be seen rolling around in it. Some cat toys have catnip inside them because cats love it so much.

People can enjoy catnip, too. Some people make catnip tea with the leaves of the plant. It is like the mint with which people make tea.

Another refreshing drink can be made with the berries of the sumac bush or tree. Native Americans would pick the red berries, crush them, and add water to make a thirst-quenching drink. The berries were sour, but they must have believed that the cool, tart drink was refreshing. Does this remind you of lemonade?

Directions: Answer these questions about unusual plants.

1. What is the main idea of the first two paragraphs above?
   Cats and people can both enjoy catnip.

2. Write two ways cats show that they love catnip.
   1) by rolling around in it
   2) by playing with a catnip toy

3. How can people use catnip?
   They can make tea with it.

50

Master Skills Reading Comprehension Grade 3

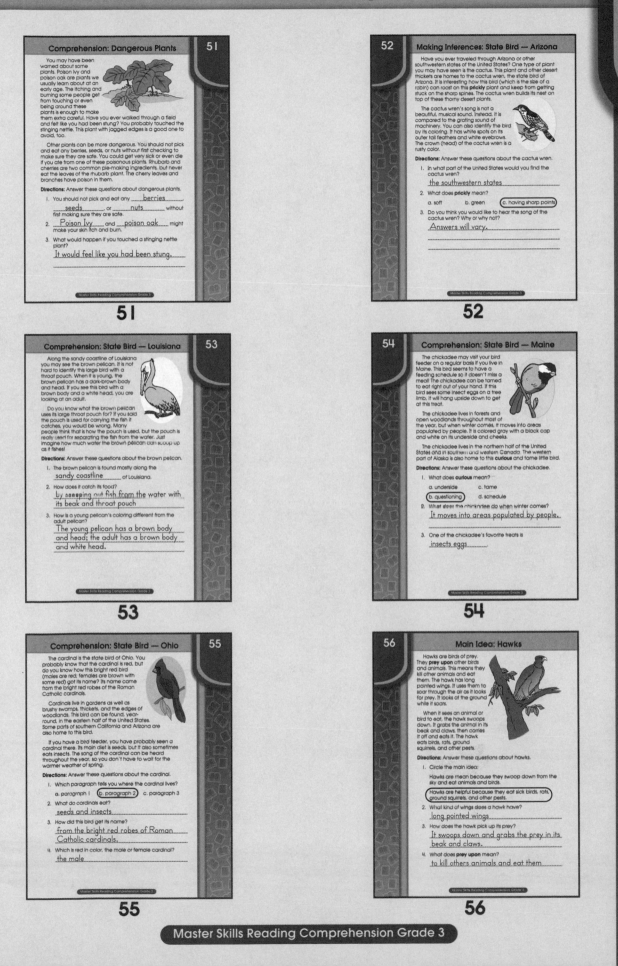

51

Comprehension: Dangerous Plants

You may have been warned about some plants. Poison ivy and poison oak are plants we usually learn about at an early age. The itching and burning some people get from touching or even being around these plants is enough to make them extra careful. Have you ever walked through a field and felt like you had been stung? You probably touched the stinging nettle. This plant with jagged edges is a good one to avoid, too.

Other plants can be more dangerous. You should not pick and eat any berries, seeds, or nuts without first checking to make sure they are safe. You could get very sick or even die if you ate from one of these poisonous plants. Rhubarb and cherries are two common pie-making ingredients, but never eat the leaves of the rhubarb plant. The cherry leaves and branches have poison in them.

Directions: Answer these questions about dangerous plants.

1. You should not pick and eat any ___berries___, ___seeds___, or ___nuts___ without first making sure they are safe.

2. ___Poison Ivy___ and ___poison oak___ might make your skin itch and burn.

3. What would happen if you touched a stinging nettle plant?
   ___It would feel like you had been stung.___

51

52

Making Inferences: State Bird — Arizona

Have you ever traveled through Arizona or other southwestern states of the United States? One type of plant you may have seen is the cactus. This plant and other desert thickets are homes to the cactus wren, the state bird of Arizona. It is interesting how this bird (which is the size of a robin) can roost on this **prickly** plant and keep from getting stuck on the sharp spines. The cactus wren builds its nest on top of these thorny desert plants.

The cactus wren's song is not a beautiful, musical sound. Instead, it is compared to the grating sound of machinery. You can also identify the bird by its coloring. It has white spots on its outer tail feathers and white eyebrows. The crown (head) of the cactus wren is a rusty color.

Directions: Answer these questions about the cactus wren.

1. In what part of the United States would you find the cactus wren?
   ___the southwestern states___

2. What does **prickly** mean?
   a. soft   b. green   (c. having sharp points)

3. Do you think you would like to hear the song of the cactus wren? Why or why not?
   ___Answers will vary.___

52

53

Comprehension: State Bird — Louisiana

Along the sandy coastline of Louisiana you may see the brown pelican. It is not hard to identify this large bird with a throat pouch. When it is young, the brown pelican has a dark-brown body and head. If you see this bird with a brown body and a white head, you are looking at an adult.

Do you know what the brown pelican uses its large throat pouch for? If you said the pouch is used for carrying the fish it catches, you would be wrong. Many people think that is how the pouch is used, but the pouch is really used for separating the fish from the water. Just imagine how much water the brown pelican can scoop up as it fishes!

Directions: Answer these questions about the brown pelican.

1. The brown pelican is found mostly along the ___sandy coastline___ of Louisiana.

2. How does it catch its food?
   ___by scooping out fish from the water with its beak and throat pouch___

3. How is a young pelican's coloring different from the adult pelican?
   ___The young pelican has a brown body and head; the adult has a brown body and white head.___

53

54

Comprehension: State Bird — Maine

The chickadee may visit your bird feeder on a regular basis if you live in Maine. This bird seems to have a feeding schedule so it doesn't miss a meal! The chickadee can be tamed to eat right out of your hand. If this bird sees some insect eggs on a tree limb, it will hang upside down to get at this treat.

The chickadee lives in forests and open woodlands throughout most of the year, but when winter comes, it moves into areas populated by people. It is colored gray with a black cap and white on its underside and cheeks.

The chickadee lives in the northern half of the United States and in southern and western Canada. The western part of Alaska is also home to this **curious** and tame little bird.

Directions: Answer these questions about the chickadee.

1. What does **curious** mean?
   a. underside   c. tame
   (b. questioning)   d. schedule

2. What does the chickadee do when winter comes?
   ___It moves into areas populated by people.___

3. One of the chickadee's favorite treats is ___insects eggs___.

54

55

Comprehension: State Bird — Ohio

The cardinal is the state bird of Ohio. You probably know that the cardinal is red, but do you know how this bright red bird (males are red; females are brown with some red) got its name? Its name came from the bright red robes of the Roman Catholic cardinals.

Cardinals live in gardens as well as brushy swamps, thickets, and the edges of woodlands. This bird can be found year-round, in the eastern half of the United States. Some parts of southern California and Arizona are also home to this bird.

If you have a bird feeder, you have probably seen a cardinal there. Its main diet is seeds, but it also sometimes eats insects. The song of the cardinal can be heard throughout the year, so you don't have to wait for the warmer weather of spring.

Directions: Answer these questions about the cardinal.

1. Which paragraph tells you where the cardinal lives?
   a. paragraph 1   (b. paragraph 2)   c. paragraph 3

2. What do cardinals eat?
   ___seeds and insects___

3. How did this bird get its name?
   ___from the bright red robes of Roman Catholic cardinals.___

4. Which is red in color, the male or female cardinal?
   ___the male___

55

56

Main Idea: Hawks

Hawks are birds of prey. They **prey upon** other birds and animals. This means they kill other animals and eat them. The hawk has long pointed wings. It uses them to soar through the air as it looks for prey. It looks at the ground while it soars.

When it sees an animal or bird to eat, the hawk swoops down. It grabs the animal in its beak and claws, then carries it off and eats it. The hawk eats birds, rats, ground squirrels, and other pests.

Directions: Answer these questions about hawks.

1. Circle the main idea:
   Hawks are mean because they swoop down from the sky and eat animals and birds.
   (Hawks are helpful because they eat sick birds, rats, ground squirrels, and other pests.)

2. What kind of wings does a hawk have?
   ___long pointed wings___

3. How does the hawk pick up its prey?
   ___It swoops down and grabs the prey in its beak and claws.___

4. What does **prey upon** mean?
   ___to kill others animals and eat them___

56

Answer Key

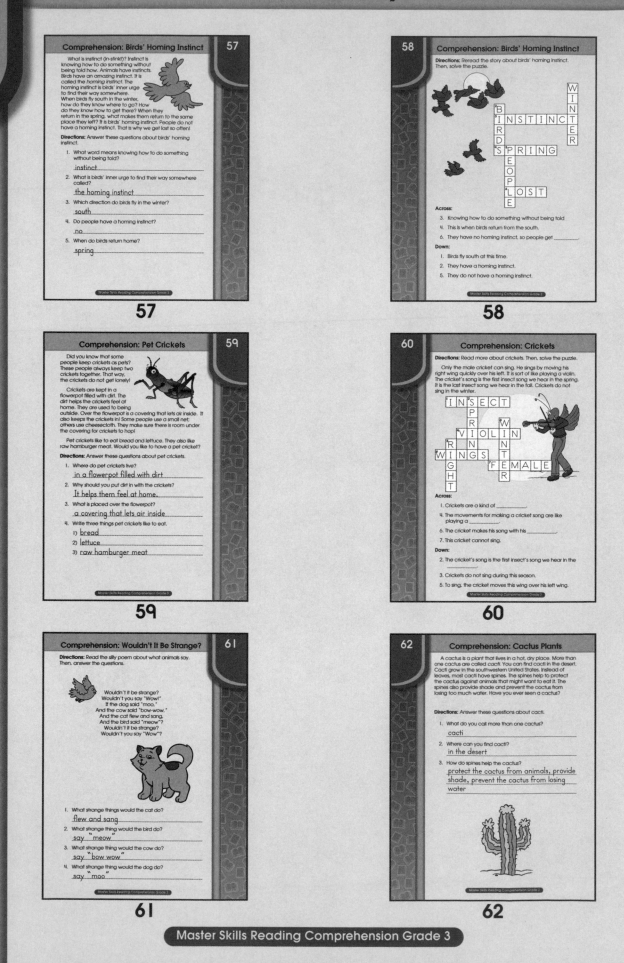

Comprehension: Birds' Homing Instinct 57

What is instinct (in-stinkt)? Instinct is knowing how to do something without being told how. Animals have instincts. Birds have an amazing instinct. It is called the *homing instinct*. The homing instinct is birds' inner urge to find their way somewhere. When birds fly south in the winter, how do they know where to go? How do they know how to get there? When they return in the spring, what makes them return to the same place they left? It is birds' homing instinct. People do not have a homing instinct. That is why we get lost so often!

Directions: Answer these questions about birds' homing instinct.

1. What word means knowing how to do something without being told?
   instinct

2. What is birds' inner urge to find their way somewhere called?
   the homing instinct

3. Which direction do birds fly in the winter?
   south

4. Do people have a homing instinct?
   no

5. When do birds return home?
   spring

57

---

58 **Comprehension: Birds' Homing Instinct**

Directions: Reread the story about birds' homing instinct. Then, solve the puzzle.

(crossword puzzle: WINTER, BIRDS, INSTINCT, SPRING, PEOPLE, LOST)

Across:
3. Knowing how to do something without being told
4. This is when birds return from the south.
6. They have no homing instinct, so people get _____.

Down:
1. Birds fly south at this time.
2. They have a homing instinct.
5. They do not have a homing instinct.

58

Comprehension: Pet Crickets 59

Did you know that some people keep crickets as pets? These people always keep two crickets together. That way, the crickets do not get lonely!

Crickets are kept in a flowerpot filled with dirt. The dirt helps the crickets feel at home. They are used to being outside. Over the flowerpot is a covering that lets air inside. It also keeps the crickets in! Some people use a small net; others use cheesecloth. They make sure there is room under the covering for crickets to hop!

Pet crickets like to eat bread and lettuce. They also like raw hamburger meat. Would you like to have a pet cricket?

Directions: Answer these questions about pet crickets.

1. Where do pet crickets live?
   in a flowerpot filled with dirt

2. Why should you put dirt in with the crickets?
   It helps them feel at home.

3. What is placed over the flowerpot?
   a covering that lets air inside

4. Write three things pet crickets like to eat.
   1) bread
   2) lettuce
   3) raw hamburger meat

59

---

60 **Comprehension: Crickets**

Directions: Read more about crickets. Then, solve the puzzle.

Only the male cricket can sing. He sings by moving his right wing quickly over his left. It is sort of like playing a violin. The cricket's song is the first insect song we hear in the spring. It is the last insect song we hear in the fall. Crickets do not sing in the winter.

(crossword puzzle: INSECT, SPRING, VIOLIN, WINTER, RIGHT, WINGS, FEMALE)

Across:
1. Crickets are a kind of _____.
4. The movements for making a cricket song are like playing a _____.
6. The cricket makes his song with his _____.
7. This cricket cannot sing.

Down:
2. The cricket's song is the first insect's song we hear in the _____.
3. Crickets do not sing during this season.
5. To sing, the cricket moves this wing over his left wing.

60

Comprehension: Wouldn't It Be Strange? 61

Directions: Read the silly poem about what animals say. Then, answer the questions.

Wouldn't it be strange?
Wouldn't you say "Wow!"
If the dog said "moo,"
And the cow said "bow-wow."
And the cat flew and sang.
And the bird said "meow"?
Wouldn't it be strange?
Wouldn't you say "Wow"?

1. What strange things would the cat do?
   flew and sang

2. What strange thing would the bird do?
   say "meow"

3. What strange thing would the cow do?
   say "bow wow"

4. What strange thing would the dog do?
   say "moo"

61

---

62 **Comprehension: Cactus Plants**

A cactus is a plant that lives in a hot, dry place. More than one cactus are called cacti. You can find cacti in the desert. Cacti grow in the southwestern United States. Instead of leaves, most cacti have spines. The spines help to protect the cactus against animals that might want to eat it. The spines also provide shade and prevent the cactus from losing too much water. Have you ever seen a cactus?

Directions: Answer these questions about cacti.

1. What do you call more than one cactus?
   cacti

2. Where can you find cacti?
   in the desert

3. How do spines help the cactus?
   protect the cactus from animals, provide shade, prevent the cactus from losing water

62

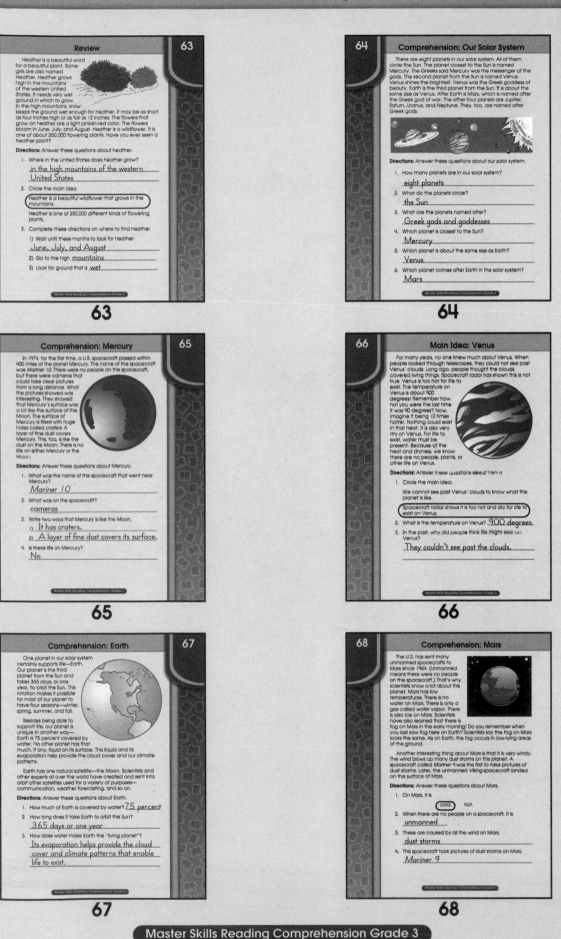

63 — Review

Heather is a beautiful word for a beautiful plant. Some girls are also named Heather. Heather grows high in the mountains of the western United States. It needs very wet ground in which to grow. In the high mountains, snow keeps the ground wet enough for heather. It may be as short as four inches high or as tall as 12 inches. The flowers that grow on heather are a light pinkish-red color. The flowers bloom in June, July, and August. Heather is a wildflower. It is one of about 250,000 flowering plants. Have you ever seen a heather plant?

Directions: Answer these questions about heather.

1. Where in the United States does heather grow?
   in the high mountains of the western United States

2. Circle the main idea:
   (Heather is a beautiful wildflower that grows in the mountains.)

   Heather is one of 250,000 different kinds of flowering plants.

3. Complete these directions on where to find heather.
   1) Wait until these months to look for heather:
      June, July, and August
   2) Go to the high mountains
   3) Look for ground that is wet

64 — Comprehension: Our Solar System

There are eight planets in our solar system. All of them circle the Sun. The planet closest to the Sun is named Mercury. The Greeks said Mercury was the messenger of the gods. The second planet from the Sun is named Venus. Venus shines the brightest. Venus was the Greek goddess of beauty. Earth is the third planet from the Sun. It is about the same size as Venus. After Earth is Mars, which is named after the Greek god of war. The other four planets are Jupiter, Saturn, Uranus, and Neptune. They, too, are named after Greek gods.

Directions: Answer these questions about our solar system.

1. How many planets are in our solar system?
   eight planets

2. What do the planets circle?
   the Sun

3. What are the planets named after?
   Greek gods and goddesses

4. Which planet is closest to the Sun?
   Mercury

5. Which planet is about the same size as Earth?
   Venus

6. Which planet comes after Earth in the solar system?
   Mars

65 — Comprehension: Mercury

In 1974, for the first time, a U.S. spacecraft passed within 400 miles of the planet Mercury. The name of the spacecraft was Mariner 10. There were no people on the spacecraft, but there were cameras that could take clear pictures from a long distance. What the pictures showed was interesting. They showed that Mercury's surface was a lot like the surface of the Moon. The surface of Mercury is filled with huge holes called craters. A layer of fine dust covers Mercury. This, too, is like the dust on the Moon. There is no life on either Mercury or the Moon.

Directions: Answer these questions about Mercury.

1. What was the name of the spacecraft that went near Mercury?
   Mariner 10

2. What was on the spacecraft?
   cameras

3. Write two ways that Mercury is like the Moon.
   1) It has craters.
   2) A layer of fine dust covers its surface.

4. Is there life on Mercury?
   No

66 — Main Idea: Venus

For many years, no one knew much about Venus. When people looked through telescopes, they could not see past Venus' clouds. Long ago, people thought the clouds covered living things. Spacecraft radar has shown this is not true. Venus is too hot for life to exist. The temperature on Venus is about 900 degrees! Remember how hot you were the last time it was 90 degrees? Now, imagine it being 10 times hotter. Nothing could exist in that heat. It is also very dry on Venus. For life to exist, water must be present. Because of the heat and dryness, we know there are no people, plants, or other life on Venus.

Directions: Answer these questions about Venus.

1. Circle the main idea:
   We cannot see past Venus' clouds to know what the planet is like.

   (Spacecraft radar shows it is too hot and dry for life to exist on Venus.)

2. What is the temperature on Venus? 900 degrees

3. In the past, why did people think life might exist on Venus?
   They couldn't see past the clouds.

67 — Comprehension: Earth

One planet in our solar system certainly supports life—Earth. Our planet is the third planet from the Sun and takes 365 days, or one year, to orbit the Sun. This rotation makes it possible for most of our planet to have four seasons—winter, spring, summer, and fall.

Besides being able to support life, our planet is unique in another way—Earth is 75 percent covered by water. No other planet has that much, if any, liquid on its surface. This liquid and its evaporation help provide the cloud cover and our climate patterns.

Earth has one natural satellite—the Moon. Scientists and other experts all over the world have created and sent into orbit other satellites used for a variety of purposes—communication, weather forecasting, and so on.

Directions: Answer these questions about Earth.

1. How much of Earth is covered by water? 75 percent

2. How long does it take Earth to orbit the Sun?
   365 days or one year

3. How does water make Earth the "living planet"?
   Its evaporation helps provide the cloud cover and climate patterns that enable life to exist.

68 — Comprehension: Mars

The U.S. has sent many unmanned spacecrafts to Mars since 1964. (Unmanned means there were no people on the spacecraft.) That's why scientists know a lot about this planet. Mars has low temperatures. There is no water on Mars. There is only a gas called water vapor. There is also ice on Mars. Scientists have also learned that there is fog on Mars in the early morning! Do you remember when you last saw fog here on Earth? Scientists say the fog on Mars looks the same. As on Earth, the fog occurs in low-lying areas of the ground.

Another interesting thing about Mars is that it is very windy. The wind blows up many dust storms on this planet. A spacecraft called Mariner 9 was the first to take pictures of dust storms. Later, the unmanned Viking spacecraft landed on the surface of Mars.

Directions: Answer these questions about Mars.

1. On Mars, it is
   (cold.) hot.

2. When there are no people on a spacecraft, it is
   unmanned

3. These are caused by all the wind on Mars.
   dust storms

4. This spacecraft took pictures of dust storms on Mars.
   Mariner 9

Answer Key

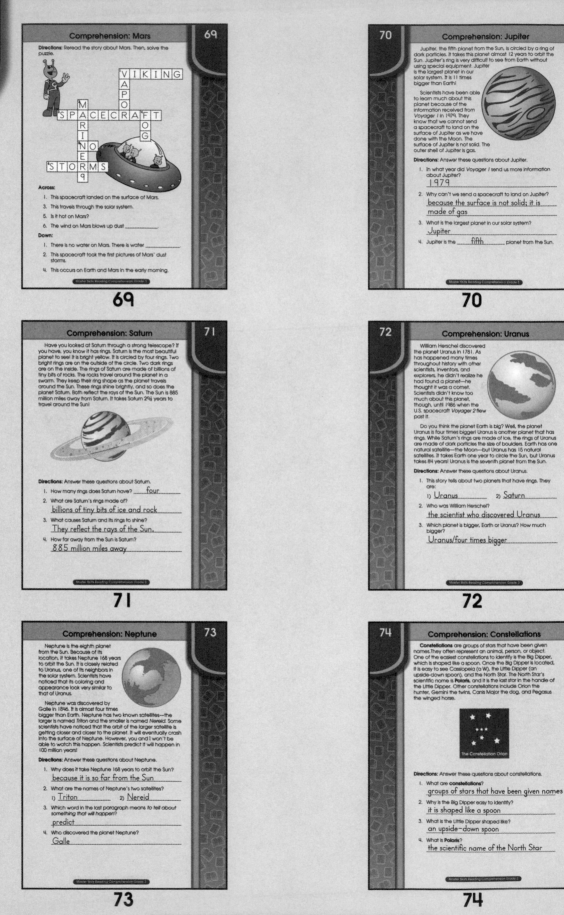

69 — Comprehension: Mars

Directions: Reread the story about Mars. Then, solve the puzzle.

Crossword answers: VIKING, VAPOR, MARINER, FOG, SPACECRAFT, STORMS

Across:
1. This spacecraft landed on the surface of Mars.
3. This travels through the solar system.
5. Is it hot on Mars?
6. The wind on Mars blows up dust _____.

Down:
1. There is no water on Mars. There is water _____.
2. This spacecraft took the first pictures of Mars' dust storms.
4. This occurs on Earth and Mars in the early morning.

70 — Comprehension: Jupiter

Jupiter, the fifth planet from the Sun, is circled by a ring of dark particles. It takes this planet almost 12 years to orbit the Sun. Jupiter's ring is very difficult to see from Earth without using special equipment. Jupiter is the largest planet in our solar system. It is 11 times bigger than Earth!

Scientists have been able to learn much about this planet because of the information received from *Voyager I* in 1979. They know that we cannot send a spacecraft to land on the surface of Jupiter as we have done with the Moon. The surface of Jupiter is not solid. The outer shell of Jupiter is gas.

Directions: Answer these questions about Jupiter.

1. In what year did *Voyager I* send us more information about Jupiter?
   1979
2. Why can't we send a spacecraft to land on Jupiter?
   because the surface is not solid; it is made of gas
3. What is the largest planet in our solar system?
   Jupiter
4. Jupiter is the **fifth** planet from the Sun.

71 — Comprehension: Saturn

Have you looked at Saturn through a strong telescope? If you have, you know it has rings. Saturn is the most beautiful planet to see! It is bright yellow. It is circled by four rings. Two bright rings are on the outside of the circle. Two dark rings are on the inside. The rings of Saturn are made of billions of tiny bits of rocks. The rocks travel around the planet in a swarm. They keep their ring shape as the planet travels around the Sun. These rings shine brightly, and so does the planet Saturn. Both reflect the rays of the Sun. The Sun is 885 million miles away from Saturn. It takes Saturn 29½ years to travel around the Sun!

Directions: Answer these questions about Saturn.

1. How many rings does Saturn have? **four**
2. What are Saturn's rings made of?
   billions of tiny bits of ice and rock
3. What causes Saturn and its rings to shine?
   They reflect the rays of the Sun.
4. How far away from the Sun is Saturn?
   885 million miles away

72 — Comprehension: Uranus

William Herschel discovered the planet Uranus in 1781. As has happened many times throughout history with other scientists, inventors, and explorers, he didn't realize he had found a planet—he thought it was a comet. Scientists didn't know too much about this planet, though, until 1986 when the U.S. spacecraft *Voyager 2* flew past it.

Do you think the planet Earth is big? Well, the planet Uranus is four times bigger! Uranus is another planet that has rings. While Saturn's rings are made of ice, the rings of Uranus are made of dark particles the size of boulders. Earth has one natural satellite—the Moon—but Uranus has 15 natural satellites. It takes Earth one year to circle the Sun, but Uranus takes 84 years! Uranus is the seventh planet from the Sun.

Directions: Answer these questions about Uranus.

1. This story tells about two planets that have rings. They are:
   1) **Uranus**   2) **Saturn**
2. Who was William Herschel?
   the scientist who discovered Uranus
3. Which planet is bigger, Earth or Uranus? How much bigger?
   Uranus/four times bigger

73 — Comprehension: Neptune

Neptune is the eighth planet from the Sun. Because of its location, it takes Neptune 168 years to orbit the Sun. It is closely related to Uranus, one of its neighbors in the solar system. Scientists have noticed that its coloring and appearance look very similar to that of Uranus.

Neptune was discovered by Galle in 1846. It is almost four times bigger than Earth. Neptune has two known satellites—the larger is named *Triton* and the smaller is named *Nereid*. Some scientists have noticed that the orbit of the larger satellite is getting closer and closer to the planet. It will eventually crash into the surface of Neptune. However, you and I won't be able to watch this happen. Scientists predict it will happen in 100 million years!

Directions: Answer these questions about Neptune.

1. Why does it take Neptune 168 years to orbit the Sun?
   because it is so far from the Sun
2. What are the names of Neptune's two satellites?
   1) **Triton**   2) **Nereid**
3. Which word in the last paragraph means *to tell about something that will happen*?
   predict
4. Who discovered the planet Neptune?
   Galle

74 — Comprehension: Constellations

Constellations are groups of stars that have been given names. They often represent an animal, person, or object. One of the easiest constellations to identify is the Big Dipper, which is shaped like a spoon. Once the Big Dipper is located, it is easy to see Cassiopeia (a W), the Little Dipper (an upside-down spoon), and the North Star. The North Star's scientific name is **Polaris**, and it is the last star in the handle of the Little Dipper. Other constellations include Orion the hunter, Gemini the twins, Canis Major the dog, and Pegasus the winged horse.

The Constellation Orion

Directions: Answer these questions about constellations.

1. What are **constellations**?
   groups of stars that have been given names
2. Why is the Big Dipper easy to identify?
   it is shaped like a spoon
3. What is the Little Dipper shaped like?
   an upside-down spoon
4. What is **Polaris**?
   the scientific name of the North Star

Answer Key

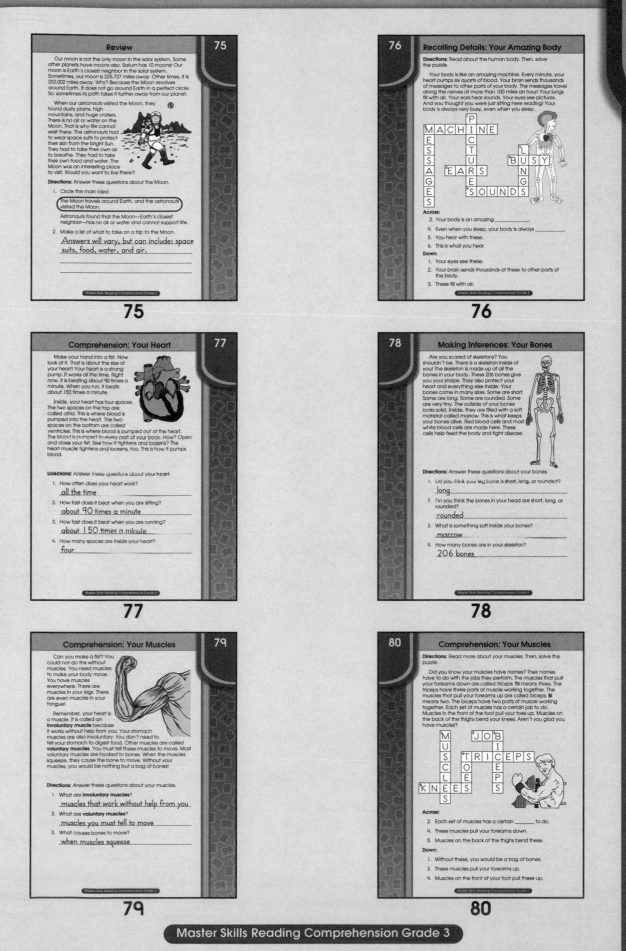

Page 75

Review

Our moon is not the only moon in the solar system. Some other planets have moons also. Saturn has 10 moons! Our moon is Earth's closest neighbor in the solar system. Sometimes, our moon is 225,727 miles away. Other times, it is 252,002 miles away. Why? Because the Moon revolves around Earth. It does not go around Earth in a perfect circle. So, sometimes its path takes it further away from our planet.

When our astronauts visited the Moon, they found dusty plains, high mountains, and huge craters. There is no air or water on the Moon. That is why life cannot exist there. The astronauts had to wear space suits to protect their skin from the bright Sun. They had to take their own air to breathe. They had to take their own food and water. The Moon was an interesting place to visit. Would you want to live there?

Directions: Answer these questions about the Moon.

1. Circle the main idea:

   (The Moon travels around Earth, and the astronauts visited the Moon.)

   Astronauts found that the Moon—Earth's closest neighbor—has no air or water and cannot support life.

2. Make a list of what to take on a trip to the Moon.

   <u>Answers will vary, but can include: space</u>
   <u>suits, food, water, and air.</u>

Page 76

Recalling Details: Your Amazing Body

Directions: Read about the human body. Then, solve the puzzle.

Your body is like an amazing machine. Every minute, your heart pumps six quarts of blood. Your brain sends thousands of messages to other parts of your body. The messages travel along the nerves at more than 100 miles an hour! Your lungs fill with air. Your ears hear sounds. Your eyes see pictures. And you thought you were just sitting here reading! Your body is always very busy, even when you sleep.

Crossword puzzle answers:
- MACHINE
- PICTURE
- MESSAGES
- BUSY
- EARS
- LUNG
- SOUNDS

Across:

2. Your body is an amazing _____.
4. Even when you sleep, your body is always _____.
5. You hear with these.
6. This is what you hear.

Down:

1. Your eyes see these.
2. Your brain sends thousands of these to other parts of the body.
3. These fill with air.

Page 77

Comprehension: Your Heart

Make your hand into a fist. Now look at it. That is about the size of your heart! Your heart is a strong pump. It works all the time. Right now, it is beating about 90 times a minute. When you run, it beats about 150 times a minute.

Inside, your heart has four spaces. The two spaces on the top are called *atria*. This is where blood is pumped into the heart. The two spaces on the bottom are called *ventricles*. This is where blood is pumped out of the heart. The blood is pumped to every part of your body. How? Open and close your fist. See how it tightens and loosens? The heart muscle tightens and loosens, too. This is how it pumps blood.

Directions: Answer these questions about your heart.

1. How often does your heart work?

   <u>all the time</u>

2. How fast does it beat when you are sitting?

   <u>about 90 times a minute</u>

3. How fast does it beat when you are running?

   <u>about 150 times a minute</u>

4. How many spaces are inside your heart?

   <u>four</u>

Page 78

Making Inferences: Your Bones

Are you scared of skeletons? You shouldn't be. There is a skeleton inside of you! The skeleton is made up of all the bones in your body. These 206 bones give you your shape. They also protect your heart and everything else inside. Your bones come in many sizes. Some are short. Some are long. Some are rounded. Some are very tiny. The outside of your bones looks solid. Inside, they are filled with a soft material called marrow. This is what keeps your bones alive. Red blood cells and most white blood cells are made here. These cells help feed the body and fight disease.

Directions: Answer these questions about your bones.

1. Do you think your leg bone is short, long, or rounded?

   <u>long</u>

2. Do you think the bones in your head are short, long, or rounded?

   <u>rounded</u>

3. What is something soft inside your bones?

   <u>marrow</u>

4. How many bones are in your skeleton?

   <u>206 bones</u>

Page 79

Comprehension: Your Muscles

Can you make a fist? You could not do this without muscles. You need muscles to make your body move. You have muscles everywhere. There are muscles in your legs. There are even muscles in your tongue!

Remember, your heart is a muscle. It is called an **involuntary muscle** because it works without help from you. Your stomach muscles are also involuntary. You don't need to tell your stomach to digest food. Other muscles are called **voluntary muscles**. You must tell these muscles to move. Most voluntary muscles are hooked to bones. When these muscles squeeze, they cause the bone to move. Without your muscles, you would be nothing but a bag of bones!

Directions: Answer these questions about your muscles.

1. What are **involuntary muscles**?

   <u>muscles that work without help from you</u>

2. What are **voluntary muscles**?

   <u>muscles you must tell to move</u>

3. What causes bones to move?

   <u>when muscles squeeze</u>

Page 80

Comprehension: Your Muscles

Directions: Read more about your muscles. Then, solve the puzzle.

Did you know your muscles have names? Their names have to do with the jobs they perform. The muscles that pull your forearms down are called *triceps*. Tri means three. The triceps have three parts of muscle working together. The muscles that pull your forearms up are called *biceps*. Bi means two. The biceps have two parts of muscle working together. Each set of muscles has a certain job to do. Muscles in the front of the foot pull your toes up. Muscles on the back of the thighs bend your knees. Aren't you glad you have muscles?

Crossword puzzle answers:
- MUSCLES
- JOB
- BICEPS
- TRICEPS
- TOES
- KNEES

Across:

2. Each set of muscles has a certain _____ to do.
4. These muscles pull your forearms down.
5. Muscles on the back of the thighs bend these.

Down:

1. Without these, you would be a bag of bones.
3. These muscles pull your forearms up.
4. Muscles on the front of your foot pull these up.

Answer Key

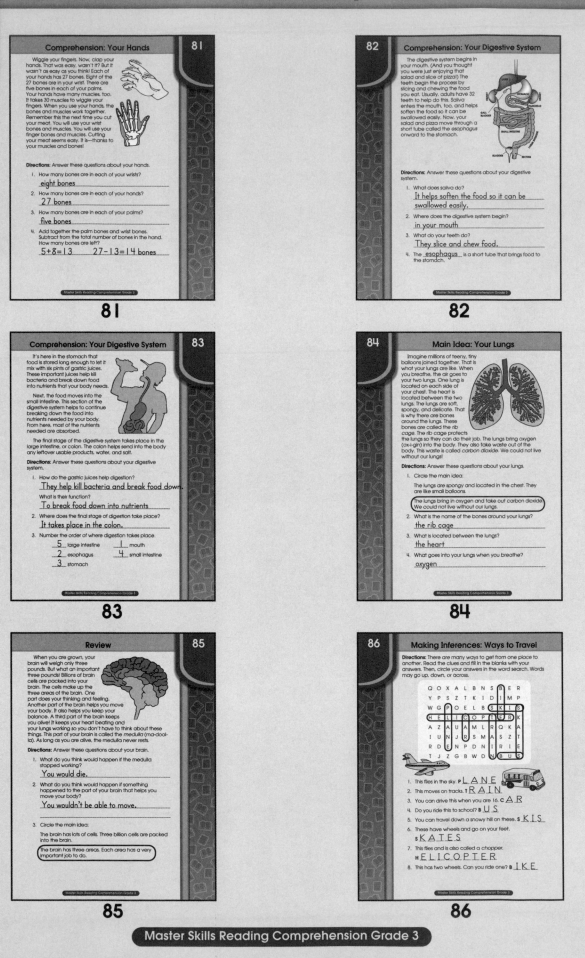

81

Comprehension: Your Hands

Wiggle your fingers. Now, clap your hands. That was easy, wasn't it? But it wasn't as easy as you think! Each of your hands has 27 bones. Eight of the 27 bones are in your wrist. There are five bones in each of your palms. Your hands have many muscles, too. It takes 30 muscles to wiggle your fingers. When you use your hands, the bones and muscles work together. Remember this the next time you cut your meat. You will use your wrist bones and muscles. You will use your finger bones and muscles. Cutting your meat seems easy. It is—thanks to your muscles and bones!

Directions: Answer these questions about your hands.

1. How many bones are in each of your wrists?
   eight bones

2. How many bones are in each of your hands?
   27 bones

3. How many bones are in each of your palms?
   five bones

4. Add together the palm bones and wrist bones. Subtract from the total number of bones in the hand. How many bones are left?
   5+8=13   27-13=14 bones

82

Comprehension: Your Digestive System

The digestive system begins in your mouth. (And you thought you were just enjoying that salad and slice of pizza!) The teeth begin the process by slicing and chewing the food you eat. Usually, adults have 32 teeth to help do this. Saliva enters the mouth, too, and helps soften the food so it can be swallowed easily. Now, your salad and pizza move through a short tube called the esophagus onward to the stomach.

Directions: Answer these questions about your digestive system.

1. What does saliva do?
   It helps soften the food so it can be swallowed easily.

2. Where does the digestive system begin?
   in your mouth

3. What do your teeth do?
   They slice and chew food.

4. The esophagus is a short tube that brings food to the stomach.

83

Comprehension: Your Digestive System

It's here in the stomach that food is stored long enough to let it mix with six pints of gastric juices. These important juices help kill bacteria and break down food into nutrients that your body needs.

Next, the food moves into the small intestine. This section of the digestive system helps to continue breaking down the food into nutrients needed by your body. From here, most of the nutrients needed are absorbed.

The final stage of the digestive system takes place in the large intestine, or colon. The colon helps send into the body any leftover usable products, water, and salt.

Directions: Answer these questions about your digestive system.

1. How do the gastric juices help digestion?
   They help kill bacteria and break food down.
   What is their function?
   To break food down into nutrients

2. Where does the final stage of digestion take place?
   It takes place in the colon.

3. Number the order of where digestion takes place.
   5 large intestine   1 mouth
   2 esophagus   4 small intestine
   3 stomach

84

Main Idea: Your Lungs

Imagine millions of teeny, tiny balloons joined together. That is what your lungs are like. When you breathe, the air goes to your two lungs. One lung is located on each side of your chest. The heart is located between the two lungs. The lungs are soft, spongy, and delicate. That is why there are bones around the lungs. These bones are called the rib cage. The rib cage protects the lungs so they can do their job. The lungs bring oxygen (ox-i-gin) into the body. They also take waste out of the body. This waste is called carbon dioxide. We could not live without our lungs!

Directions: Answer these questions about your lungs.

1. Circle the main idea:
   The lungs are spongy and located in the chest. They are like small balloons.
   (The lungs bring in oxygen and take out carbon dioxide. We could not live without our lungs.)

2. What is the name of the bones around your lungs?
   the rib cage

3. What is located between the lungs?
   the heart

4. What goes into your lungs when you breathe?
   oxygen

85

Review

When you are grown, your brain will weigh only three pounds. But what an important three pounds! Billions of brain cells are packed into your brain. The cells make up the three areas of the brain. One part does your thinking and feeling. Another part of the brain helps you move your body. It also helps you keep your balance. A third part of the brain keeps you alive! It keeps your heart beating and your lungs working so you don't have to think about these things. This part of your brain is called the medulla (ma-dool-la). As long as you are alive, the medulla never rests.

Directions: Answer these questions about your brain.

1. What do you think would happen if the medulla stopped working?
   You would die.

2. What do you think would happen if something happened to the part of your brain that helps you move your body?
   You wouldn't be able to move.

3. Circle the main idea:
   The brain has lots of cells. Three billion cells are packed into the brain.
   (The brain has three areas. Each area has a very important job to do.)

86

Making Inferences: Ways to Travel

Directions: There are many ways to get from one place to another. Read the clues and fill in the blanks with your answers. Then, circle your answers in the word search. Words may go up, down, or across.

```
Q O X A L B N S B E R
Y P S Z T K I D I M P
W G P O E L B S K I S
H E L I C O P T E R K
A Z A U A M L R Q K A
I U N J R S M A S Z T
R D E N P D N I R I E
T J Z G B W D N B U S
```

1. This flies in the sky. P L A N E
2. This moves on tracks. T R A I N
3. You can drive this when you are 16. C A R
4. Do you ride this to school? B U S
5. You can travel down a snowy hill on these. S K I S
6. These have wheels and go on your feet. S K A T E S
7. This flies and is also called a chopper. H E L I C O P T E R
8. This has two wheels. Can you ride one? B I K E

Answer Key

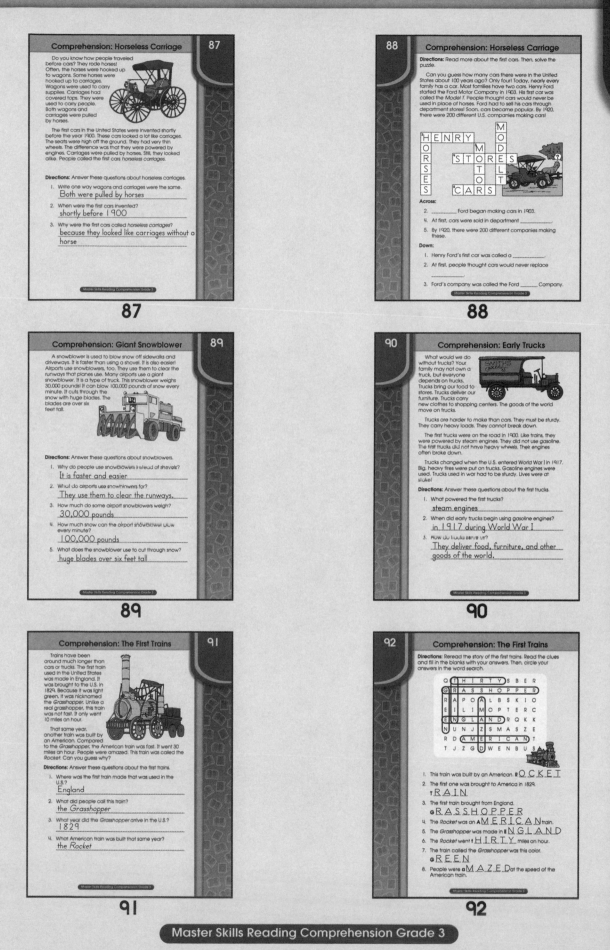

Page 87 — Comprehension: Horseless Carriage

Do you know how people traveled before cars? They rode horses! Often, the horses were hooked up to wagons. Some horses were hooked up to carriages. Wagons were used to carry supplies. Carriages had covered tops. They were used to carry people. Both wagons and carriages were pulled by horses.

The first cars in the United States were invented shortly before the year 1900. These cars looked a lot like carriages. The seats were high off the ground. They had very thin wheels. The difference was that they were powered by engines. Carriages were pulled by horses. Still, they looked alike. People called the first cars *horseless carriages*.

Directions: Answer these questions about horseless carriages.

1. Write one way wagons and carriages were the same.
   Both were pulled by horses

2. When were the first cars invented?
   shortly before 1900

3. Why were the first cars called *horseless carriages*?
   because they looked like carriages without a horse

Page 88 — Comprehension: Horseless Carriage

Directions: Read more about the first cars. Then, solve the puzzle.

Can you guess how many cars there were in the United States about 100 years ago? Only four! Today, nearly every family has a car. Most families have two cars. Henry Ford started the Ford Motor Company in 1903. His first car was called the *Model T*. People thought cars would never be used in place of horses. Ford had to sell his cars through department stores! Soon, cars became popular. By 1920, there were 200 different U.S. companies making cars!

Crossword:
HENRY / HORSES / MODEL T / STORES / MOTOR / CARS

Across:

2. _____ Ford began making cars in 1903.
4. At first, cars were sold in department _____.
5. By 1920, there were 200 different companies making these.

Down:

1. Henry Ford's first car was called a _____.
2. At first, people thought cars would never replace _____.
3. Ford's company was called the Ford _____ Company.

Page 89 — Comprehension: Giant Snowblower

A snowblower is used to blow snow off sidewalks and driveways. It is faster than using a shovel. It is also easier! Airports use snowblowers, too. They use them to clear the runways that planes use. Many airports use a giant snowblower. It is a type of truck. This snowblower weighs 30,000 pounds! It can blow 100,000 pounds of snow every minute. It cuts through the snow with huge blades. The blades are over six feet tall.

Directions: Answer these questions about snowblowers.

1. Why do people use snowblowers instead of shovels?
   It is faster and easier

2. What do airports use snowblowers for?
   They use them to clear the runways.

3. How much do some airport snowblowers weigh?
   30,000 pounds

4. How much snow can the airport snowblower blow every minute?
   100,000 pounds

5. What does the snowblower use to cut through snow?
   huge blades over six feet tall

Page 90 — Comprehension: Early Trucks

What would we do without trucks? Your family may not own a truck, but everyone depends on trucks. Trucks bring our food to stores. Trucks deliver our furniture. Trucks carry new clothes to shopping centers. The goods of the world move on trucks.

Trucks are harder to make than cars. They must be sturdy. They carry heavy loads. They cannot break down.

The first trucks were on the road in 1900. Like trains, they were powered by steam engines. They did not use gasoline. The first trucks did not have heavy wheels. Their engines often broke down.

Trucks changed when the U.S. entered World War I in 1917. Big, heavy tires were put on trucks. Gasoline engines were used. Trucks used in war had to be sturdy. Lives were at stake!

Directions: Answer these questions about the first trucks.

1. What powered the first trucks?
   steam engines

2. When did early trucks begin using gasoline engines?
   in 1917 during World War I

3. How do trucks serve us?
   They deliver food, furniture, and other goods of the world.

Page 91 — Comprehension: The First Trains

Trains have been around much longer than cars or trucks. The first train used in the United States was made in England. It was brought to the U.S. in 1829. Because it was light green, it was nicknamed the *Grasshopper*. Unlike a real grasshopper, this train was not fast. It only went 10 miles an hour.

That same year, another train was built by an American. Compared to the *Grasshopper*, the American train was fast. It went 30 miles an hour. People were amazed. This train was called the *Rocket*. Can you guess why?

Directions: Answer these questions about the first trains.

1. Where was the first train made that was used in the U.S.?
   England

2. What did people call this train?
   the *Grasshopper*

3. What year did the *Grasshopper* arrive in the U.S.?
   1829

4. What American train was built that same year?
   the *Rocket*

Page 92 — Comprehension: The First Trains

Directions: Reread the story of the first trains. Read the clues and fill in the blanks with your answers. Then, circle your answers in the word search.

Word search grid:
G T H I R T Y S B E R
G R A S S H O P P E R
R A P O A L B S K I O
E I L I M O P T E R C
E N G L A N D R Q K K
N U N J Z S M A S Z E
R D A M E R I C A N T
T J Z G D W E N B U S A

1. This train was built by an American. R O C K E T
2. The first one was brought to America in 1829. T R A I N
3. The first train brought from England. G R A S S H O P P E R
4. The *Rocket* was an A M E R I C A N train.
5. The *Grasshopper* was made in E N G L A N D
6. The *Rocket* went T H I R T Y miles an hour.
7. The train called the *Grasshopper* was this color. G R E E N
8. People were a M A Z E D at the speed of the American train.

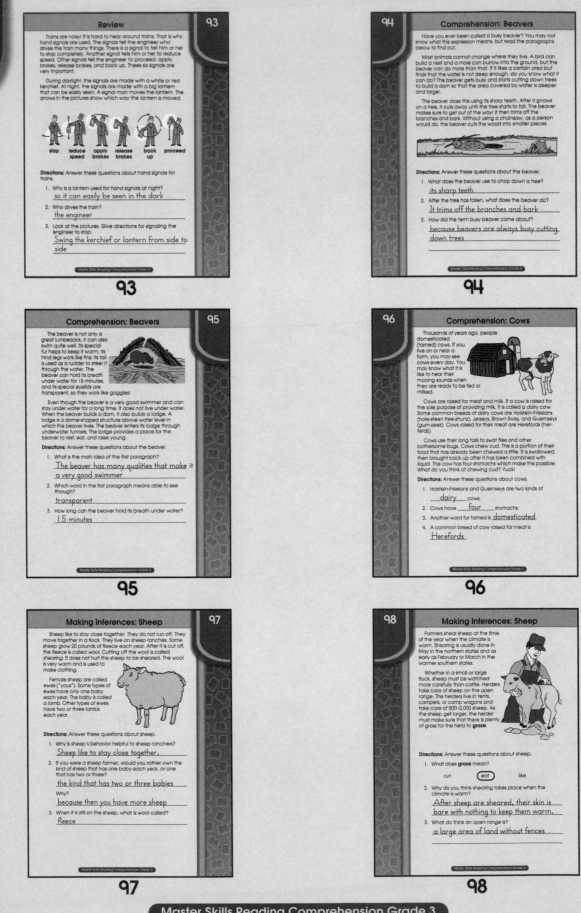

93 — Review

Trains are noisy! It is hard to hear around trains. That is why hand signals are used. The signals tell the engineer who drives the train many things. There is a signal to tell him or her to stop completely. Another signal tells him or her to reduce speed. Other signals tell the engineer to proceed, apply brakes, release brakes, and back up. These six signals are very important.

During daylight, the signals are made with a white or red kerchief. At night, the signals are made with a big lantern that can be easily seen. A signal man moves the lantern. The arrows in the pictures show which way the lantern is moved.

stop — reduce speed — apply brakes — release brakes — back up — proceed

Directions: Answer these questions about hand signals for trains.

1. Why is a lantern used for hand signals at night?
   so it can easily be seen in the dark
2. Who drives the train?
   the engineer
3. Look at the pictures. Give directions for signaling the engineer to stop.
   Swing the kerchief or lantern from side to side

94 — Comprehension: Beavers

Have you ever been called a busy beaver? You may not know what this expression means, but read the paragraphs below to find out.

Most animals cannot change where they live. A bird can build a nest and a mole can burrow into the ground, but the beaver can do more than that. If it likes a certain area but finds that the water is not deep enough, do you know what it can do? The beaver gets busy and starts cutting down trees to build a dam so that the area covered by water is deeper and larger.

The beaver does this using its sharp teeth. After it gnaws on a tree, it cuts away until the tree starts to fall. The beaver makes sure to get out of the way! It then trims off the branches and bark. Without using a chainsaw, as a person would do, the beaver cuts the wood into smaller pieces.

Directions: Answer these questions about the beaver.

1. What does the beaver use to chop down a tree?
   its sharp teeth
2. After the tree has fallen, what does the beaver do?
   It trims off the branches and bark
3. How did the term busy beaver come about?
   because beavers are always busy cutting down trees

95 — Comprehension: Beavers

The beaver is not only a great lumberjack, it can also swim quite well. Its special fur helps to keep it warm. Its hind legs work like fins. Its tail is used as a rudder to steer it through the water. The beaver can hold its breath under water for 15 minutes, and its special eyelids are transparent, so they work like goggles!

Even though the beaver is a very good swimmer and can stay under water for a long time, it does not live under water. When the beaver builds a dam, it also builds a lodge. A lodge is a dome-shaped structure above water level in which the beaver lives. The beaver enters its lodge through underwater tunnels. The lodge provides a place for the beaver to rest, eat, and raise young.

Directions: Answer these questions about the beaver.

1. What is the main idea of the first paragraph?
   The beaver has many qualities that make it a very good swimmer
2. Which word in the first paragraph means able to see through?
   transparent
3. How long can the beaver hold its breath under water?
   15 minutes

96 — Comprehension: Cows

Thousands of years ago, people domesticated (tamed) cows. If you live on or near a farm, you may see cows every day. You may know what it is like to hear their mooing sounds when they are ready to be fed or milked.

Cows are raised for meat and milk. If a cow is raised for the sole purpose of providing milk, it is called a dairy cow. Some common breeds of dairy cows are Holstein-Friesians (hole-steen free-zhunz), Jerseys, Brown Swiss, and Guernseys (gurn-zeez). Cows raised for their meat are Herefords (her-ferdz).

Cows use their long tails to swat flies and other bothersome bugs. Cows chew cud. This is a portion of their food that has already been chewed a little. It is swallowed, then brought back up after it has been combined with liquid. The cow has four stomachs which make this possible. What do you think of chewing cud? Yuck!

Directions: Answer these questions about cows.

1. Holstein-Friesians and Guernseys are two kinds of dairy cows.
2. Cows have four stomachs.
3. Another word for tamed is domesticated.
4. A common breed of cow raised for meat is Herefords.

97 — Making Inferences: Sheep

Sheep like to stay close together. They do not run off. They move together in a flock. They live on sheep ranches. Some sheep grow 20 pounds of fleece each year. After it is cut off, the fleece is called wool. Cutting off the wool is called shearing. It does not hurt the sheep to be sheared. The wool is very warm and is used to make clothing.

Female sheep are called ewes ("yous"). Some types of ewes have only one baby each year. The baby is called a lamb. Other types of ewes have two or three lambs each year.

Directions: Answer these questions about sheep.

1. Why is sheep's behavior helpful to sheep ranchers?
   Sheep like to stay close together.
2. If you were a sheep farmer, would you rather own the kind of sheep that has one baby each year, or one that has two or three?
   the kind that has two or three babies
   Why?
   because then you have more sheep
3. When it is still on the sheep, what is wool called?
   fleece

98 — Making Inferences: Sheep

Farmers shear sheep at the time of the year when the climate is warm. Shearing is usually done in May in the northern states and as early as February or March in the warmer southern states.

Whether in a small or large flock, sheep must be watched more carefully than cattle. Herders take care of sheep on the open range. The herders live in tents, campers, or camp wagons and take care of 500–2,000 sheep. As the sheep get larger, the herder must make sure that there is plenty of grass for the herd to graze.

Directions: Answer these questions about sheep.

1. What does graze mean?
   run   (eat)   like
2. Why do you think shearing takes place when the climate is warm?
   After sheep are sheared, their skin is bare with nothing to keep them warm.
3. What do think an open range is?
   a large area of land without fences

Answer Key

Comprehension: Rhinos

99

Rhinos are the second largest land animal. Only elephants are bigger.

Most people think rhinos are ugly. Their full name is rhinoceros (rhy-nos-ur-us). There are five kinds of rhinos—the square-lipped rhino, black rhino, great Indian rhino, Sumatran (sue-ma-trahn) rhino, and Javan rhino.

Rhinos have a great sense of smell, which helps protect them. They can smell other animals far away. They don't eat them, though. Rhinos do not eat meat. They are **vegetarians**.

Directions: Answer these questions about rhinos.

1. What is the largest land animal?
   the elephant
2. What are the five kinds of rhinos?
   1) square-lipped rhino
   2) black rhino
   3) great Indian rhino
   4) Sumatran rhino
   5) Javan rhino
3. What is a **vegetarian**?
   Someone who does not eat meat, only plants

99

Comprehension: Robins

100

Have you ever heard this old song? "Oh, the red, red robin goes bob-bob-bobbin' along!" It's hard not to smile when you see a robin. Robins were first called redbreasts. If you have seen one, you know why! The fronts of their bodies are red. Robins are cheerful-looking birds.

Robins sing a sweet, mellow song. That is another reason why people like robins. The female robin lays two to six eggs. She sits on them for two weeks. Then, the father and mother robin both bring food to the baby birds. Robins eat spiders, worms, insects, and small seeds. Robins will also eat food scraps people put out for them.

Directions: Answer these questions about robins.

1. Write one reason people like robins.
   Robins are cheerful-looking birds
2. How many eggs does a mother robin lay?
   two to six eggs
3. What do robins eat?
   spiders, worms, insects, small seeds, and food scraps
4. Who sits on the robin's eggs?
   the female

100

Recalling Details: Puzzle for the Birds

101

Directions: Reread the story about robins. Then, solve the puzzle.

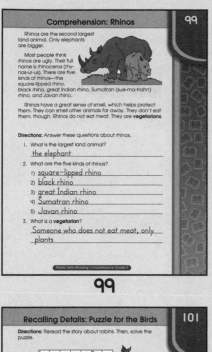

Across:

1. One type of food robins eat.
3. The mother robin lays from two to six of these.
4. Robins are _____-looking birds.
6. Another type of food robins eat.

Down:

1. The robin's _____ is sweet and mellow.
2. Robins were first called by this name.
5. Mother and father robins bring this to their babies.

101

Comprehension: Rodents

102

You are surrounded by rodents (row-dents)! There are 1,500 different kinds of rodents. One of the most common rodents is the mouse. Rats, gophers (go-furs), and beavers are also rodents. So are squirrels and porcupines (pork-you-pines).

All rodents have long, sharp teeth. These sharp teeth are called *incisors* (in-size-ors). Rodents use these teeth to eat their food. They eat mostly seeds and vegetables. There is one type of rodent some children have as a pet. No, it is not a rat! It is the guinea (ginney) pig.

Directions: Answer these questions about rodents.

1. How many different kinds of rodents are there?
   1,500
2. Name seven kinds of rodents.
   1) mice
   2) rats
   3) gophers
   4) beavers
   5) squirrels
   6) porcupines
   7) guinea pigs
3. What rodent is sometimes a pet?
   guinea pig

102

Review

103

Have you ever smelled a skunk? A skunk's odor helps protect it. The smell comes from scent glands under the skunk's tail. These scent glands make a liquid that smells very bad. The skunk can shoot the liquid 10 feet into the air. The skunk shoots this liquid to protect itself. The skunk arches it back before it shoots.

There are 10 types of skunks. The most common type is black. It has a white stripe down its head and back. It has a black tip on its tail. Some people have skunks for pets. What do you think they have to remove from the skunk before bringing it home?

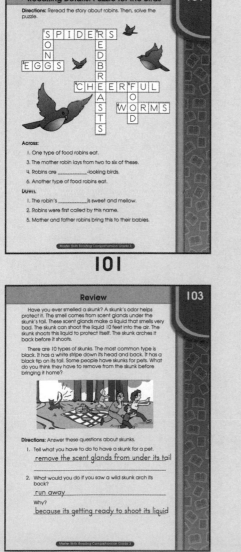

Directions: Answer these questions about skunks.

1. Tell what you have to do to have a skunk for a pet.
   remove the scent glands from under its tail

2. What would you do if you saw a wild skunk arch its back?
   run away
   Why?
   because its getting ready to shoot its liquid

103

Making Inferences: Dictionary Mystery

104

Directions: Below are six dictionary entries with pronunciations and definitions. The only things missing are the entry words. Write the correct entry words. Be sure to spell each word correctly.

Entry word:
rose
(rōz)
A flower that grows on bushes and vines.

Entry word:
rabbit
(ra bət)
A small animal that has long ears.

Entry word:
fox
(fŏks)
A wild animal that lives in the woods.

Entry word:
piano
(pē ăn ō)
A musical instrument that has many keys.

Entry word:
lake
(lāk)
A body of water that is surrounded by land.

Entry word:
baseball
(bās bôl)
A game played with a bat and a ball.

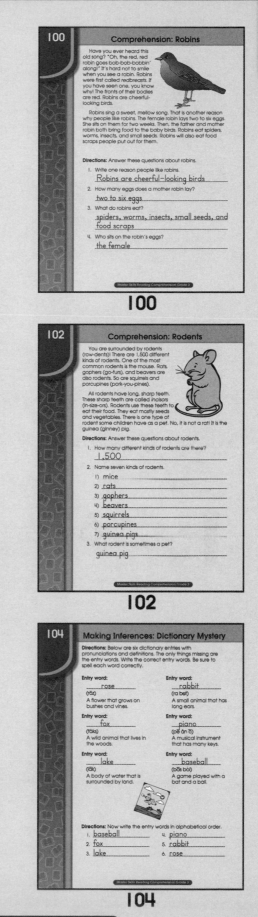

Directions: Now write the entry words in alphabetical order.

1. baseball
2. fox
3. lake
4. piano
5. rabbit
6. rose

104

105

Opposites: An Opposites Poem

Directions: Read the silly poem and then rewrite it below. As you write, change each bold word into its opposite.

In the **beautiful** land of Goop-dee-goo
Everyone eats a sweet apple stew.
The **boys walk backwards** all day long
And **whisper** when they sing a song.
The **girls** are always kind and fair.
They have **big** thumbs and **long** green hair.
It **never** rains, so **remember** that—
You **won't** need an umbrella or a hat.
Please **come** along **here** to Goop-dee-goo.
We'll all be looking **out** for you.

—*Peggy Kaye*

In the ugly land of Goop-dee-goo
No one eats a sour apple stew.
The girls run forward all day long
And yell when they sing a song.
The boys are always kind and fair.
They have small thumbs and short green hair.
It always rains, so forget that—
You will need an umbrella or a hat.
Please go along there to Goop-dee-goo.
We'll always be looking for you.

105

106

Homophones

Homophones are words that sound alike but have different meanings or spellings, such as **week** and **weak**.

The Sun and its planets move through the Milky Way. Do you know how fast the sun and planets move? To find out, follow the instructions below.

Directions: Write the correct word in each sentence. Write the number next to each word you choose in the number box, starting on the left. Add up all the numbers.

Come over **here**.	hear 10	here 20
The wind **blew** all night.	blew 25	blue 15
I can **see** you.	see 25	sea 10
That mouse has a long **tail**.	tail 15	tale 10
We **won** the race!	one 15	won 30
Look at my **new** bike.	knew 20	new 25
How much does a whale **weigh**?	weigh 20	way 15
Put the belt on your **waist**.	waste 10	waist 15

Number Box

20 + 25 + 25 + 15 + 30 + 25 + 20 + 15 = 175

Complete this sentence with the answer from the number box.

The Sun and planets travel **175** miles every second!

106

107

Homograph Puzzle

Homographs are words that are spelled the same but have different meanings or pronunciations, such as **bow** (ribbon) and **bow** (of a ship).

Directions: Think of one word that fits both sentences. Write that word in the puzzle.

Across:

2. You _____ go to the show. My birthday is on _____ 11th.
3. I _____ a bluebird. I will _____ the wood.
4. Do not _____ the bus. My teacher is _____ Jones.
5. _____ me the book. Look at the clock's big _____.
8. You have dirt on your _____. A clock has hands and a _____.
9. I will act in a _____. I want to _____ baseball.

Down:

1. Turn on the _____. The bag feels _____.
2. I know what you _____. Be nice! Don't be _____.
6. I will _____ the cards. It is a fair _____.
7. They _____ yesterday. It is in my _____ hand.
8. The bird can _____. Don't let that _____ in the house.

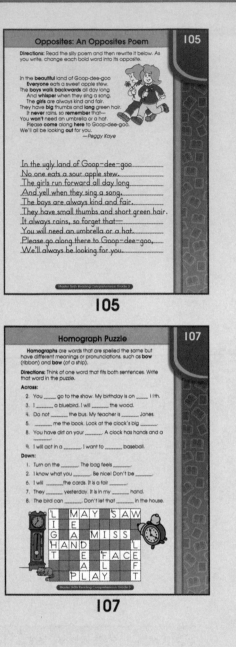

107

Comprehension

As you read with your child, encourage him or her to picture in his or her mind what is happening. This will help your child recall the story using the mind's eye as well as the ear. Ask him or her to retell the story, noting details from the beginning, middle, and end.

At this age, your child is or may soon be reading chapter books. These books have very few pictures. Check your child's comprehension by having him or her draw pictures representing the action or the problem for each chapter. Before starting each new chapter, ask your child to predict what will happen.

When you read with your child, take turns asking each other questions about the story. Your child may find it more difficult to think of a question to ask than to answer a question, so give him or her clues from the story to help.

Invite your child to write a different ending or new chapter to a story. If your child can do this in a logical manner, he or she has grasped the plot or ideas presented.

Following Directions

Your child may find it difficult to understand oral directions. This usually happens because he or she is not really listening. Make sure you have eye contact and the full attention of your child when giving directions.

Written directions need to be understood before they can be followed. Have your child read directions aloud so you can check his or her understanding before he or she attempts an activity.

Show your child the importance of following directions by preparing a simple recipe together. Point out how the steps must be followed in order. Then, invite him or her to write a recipe for making a sandwich, chocolate milk, or another simple food. Encourage your child to include all the necessary steps, then see if you can create the recipe from your child's directions.

Inference

Guide your child to figure out what an author means even when it is not directly stated in the writing. Practice by describing a situation to your child and having him or her tell you what is happening. **Example**: I got some baby shampoo and a big towel. I went into the backyard and unwound the hose and turned on the water. The dog took one look at me and tried to run out the gate. What is happening? (I am getting ready to wash the dog.)

Main Idea

Invite your child to group things into categories such as color, shape, size, or idea to see if the concept, or main idea, is understood. **Example:** round things, wild animals, sports played outside, board games.

Set up a group of items and have your child locate something else that would fit in that group. You may want to provide several items from which he or she can choose. As your child's skill level increases, invite him or her to locate something on his or her own.

Ask your child questions while reading together, such as "What is the most important thing the author is saying in this paragraph?"

Detail

Place some items on a table and give your child 10 to 30 seconds to memorize them. Then, as your child's back is turned, remove one of the items. Have your child see if he or she can tell you what is missing. Increase the difficulty by removing two or more items.

Write ideas on index cards, such as "summer vacation." Then, invite your child to write three or four details about the idea, such as "lots of fun, no school, playing with friends, camping, riding bikes", and so on.

Write a simple sentence for your child. **Example**: The cat ran down the street. Show your child how adding details makes the sentence more interesting. **Example:** The fluffy white cat ran quickly down the noisy street.

Take this idea one step further and have your child write a story about a family trip or a day at the mall, the beach, or at Grandma's. Encourage him or her to include lots of details about what happened.